The Face of the Fox

The Face of the Fox

Frederick O. Gearing

State University of New York

Buffalo

Sheffield Publishing Company
Salem, Wisconsin

For information about this book, write or call:
Sheffield Publishing Company
P.O. Box 359
9009 Antioch Road
Salem, Wisconsin 53168
(414) 843-2281

TO SOL TAX

Contents

The Face of the Fox

1. Prologue

THIS BOOK is about American Indians. It presents a selective description of one Indian community, the six hundred Fox Indians who live just outside Tama, Iowa. Besides describing the community, the study claims to diagnose its acute discomfort and to name a cure.

Around the world there are many millions of such men, the tribal peoples and rural peasants of the world. All live in very small communities, all are caught up by large social forces generated in the great societies that surround them, and all are trying to find or create for themselves some small measure of animal comfort and human dignity. Fundamentally, the Fox Indians are like those millions, the world's tribals and peasants, and Fox discomfort is not unlike theirs.

This book is also about white men; some of them are

neighbors of the Fox Indians, and one is the writer. All these white men, these men formed by the Western tradition, when they looked across at the Fox, were estranged. So one must ask: What went on inside the heads of these Western men that estranged them from the Fox? And can one do anything about it? What is the typical cause of such estrangements?

These few white men are like the many other Westerners who chance upon encounters with tribal peoples and rural peasants around the world: Peace Corpsmen, businessmen, drifters, missionaries, privates and generals, VISTA workers. Many of these, like the neighbors of the Fox and the writer, on occasion look across at some tribal or peasant others, and when they do, virtually all are estranged. *All* our children will so look across at culturally alien others, some few years hence, and virtually all will be estranged.

"Estranged," I said. Estrangement means more than feelings of contempt or indifference. It includes pity. Western men often come to their encounters with these tribal and peasant peoples wanting to love—needing to feel affection, respect, all positive things, and to express that love. These Western men come to such encounters wanting to love; they are almost always estranged; thus, wanting to love, they express their estrangement in altruistic but hurtful invidious impulses to help, even in attempts to help. Other Western men, needing to hate, feel contempt and perhaps are abusive. Still others are merely indifferent, preoccupied. Pity, contempt, indifference may be different expressions of a common underlying estrangement. *When one is estranged he is unable to relate, because he cannot see enough to relate to.* Thus the answer to what inside all those Western heads causes estrangement cannot be couched in the now familiar words ethnocentrism, cultural relativity, prejudice, and so on, which are generally taken as preachement that one should get a grip on one's emotional life. An answer, in those terms, could only affect a man's manner of expressing estrangement, could move him perhaps, from contempt to pity.

It seems plausible, however, in any event interestingly possible, that the underlying causes of estrangement are purely cognitive. Possibly certain identifiable habits of thought, wholly cognitive in nature, grip our Western minds, determine what we observe and what we fail to observe, cozen us in general and estrange us in particular, whenever we chance to look across at some tribal or peasant other.

And can one do anything about that? Possibly. One can identify and name those habits of mind; one can identify and name other devices of mind, also purely cognitive, that do better work; and one can thereby perhaps gain a measure of control over the mind, that it may cozen less. *The opposite of being estranged is to find a people believable.*

This book therefore moves back and forth, from early descriptions of the Fox community, to contemporary tracings of thought-careers as shaped by evident habits of mind then in the heads of the author and other white observers, back to those early descriptions of the community, and so on.

When one is estranged he is unable to relate, because he cannot see enough to relate to. Estrangement shackles. If the opposite of being estranged is to find a people believable, I have the conceit that this book is an exercise in liberal, that is to say, liberating, education.

2. Games That Words Play

THE QUESTION that pressed hard upon me at that time, now nearly twenty years past, was: what can you see if you look? and what can you comprehend if you think? about the life of a small place, like a community of six hundred Fox Indians, a people with very different cultural roots than my own. The question would bother anyone. To a student of anthropology, with little formal training and with no earlier field experience, being watched and tested by his intellectual superiors, the question produced no answers, only anxiety, as our small group drove from Chicago to Tama, Iowa, thence two miles west to where the dirt road turned off the highway into the Fox community.

The road running into the Fox Indian settlement was, that

July afternoon in 1952, very dusty. We turned in at the first house, the farmhouse where we, my wife and I and two fellow students of anthropology, were to stay. The car noise brought from the house the Indian family with whom we would live. Mother and Father in their thirties and two of their three young children clustered just outside the door, waiting. Our smiles were broad, theirs tentative; our eyes sought theirs without much success. I called out a very loud hello, and at this the tentative Indian smiles seemed to freeze, then fade. All of us, we and the Indians, rather awkwardly got the suitcases out of the car and into the house. Perhaps two dozen words were said. Then I went for a walk.

The unpaved road led into this small bit of Indian country, the Fox community. On the left of the road the fields were low and weedy; on the right and ahead were wooded hilly rises. Here and there, set back in small, green clearings some distance from the road, were the homes: small frame houses, generally unpainted or not recently painted; often there was a second structure a few yards away, one of the bark-covered, loaf-shaped traditional homes of these Indians, called by them "wickiups." Chevrolets and Fords, neither very new nor very ancient, frequently came down the road, passed me (Indian faces briefly visible), and disappeared behind clouds of dust. As I moved along the road, men in work clothes came occasionally into view near the distant houses, busying themselves with a dismantled car or a broken fence; each looked up briefly and returned to his work. Children were everywhere, at chores and at play. Their mothers were less often visible, hoeing in the gardens or hanging up laundry. No one more than glanced in my direction (except some very young children who simply stood and stared) and no one spoke.

On first view from the road, the Fox revealed neither prosperity nor abject poverty, neither bustling activity nor lethargy, neither beauty nor ugliness, and the people seemed neither friendly nor hostile. I retraced my steps to the farmhouse.

Other students of anthropology, like ourselves from the University of Chicago, had recently worked among the Fox: Robert Rietz, Lisa Redfield Peattie, and Walter Miller I knew well; they had first come during the summer of 1948, and they and others had spent intermittent weeks and months in the community during the ensuing three years. Two decades earlier, Sol Tax (who had arranged those visits and now our own) had done research in the community. We were automatically inheriting the social places created by these others. The farmhouse itself (recently purchased by the University) and its resident Indian family (who lived there year round by a loose, informal agreement) were parts of this legacy. Before nightfall the word would have reached the farthest corner of the community: "The students are back." Other parts of the legacy were reports written by Tax, Miller, Peattie, and Rietz, and several conversations with them. That first night was a restless one, and facts and understandings from those reports and conversations were much in mind, if only in the abstract.

During the next several days I sought out certain Indians, and we talked. Our conversations were typically low-keyed, filled with long silences; I never quite felt that I was intruding, but was never fully confident that I was not. Or, I simply noted as best I could what I chanced to see of the everyday goings and comings of the Fox in the community and in nearby Tama. Among the things I abstractly knew from those earlier reports, a few of the more gross facts were reconfirmed and thus made concretely meaningful. These Indians, who were called by others Fox, called themselves Mesquakies, which might anciently have meant "Red Earth People." They spoke Mesquakie, and all except the oldest also spoke English. They numbered about six hundred and were a growing community; in 1910 there had been only 250. They owned 3,350 acres along both sides of the meandering Iowa River, in Tama County, near the center of Iowa.

Fox men held jobs, much of the time, in factories and with construction crews in the surrounding towns and cities, within an area roughly bounded by Des Moines, Marshalltown, Waterloo, and Cedar Rapids. Fox women shopped in the supermarkets in Tama, only two miles east, population 3,000, and the Indian families went to Tama at least once a week to pick up the weekly *Tama News–Herald* and to stand at the corners in little knots, apparently talking. The children attended the early grades, preschool through eighth, in a school of fine appearance and good reputation run by the United States Bureau of Indian Affairs; or they went to the public junior and senior high schools in Tama, where many Fox boys starred in football and other sports. At the high school a certain Indianness had rubbed off on the others; for example, the name of the school teams was the Tama-Hawks.

All these superficial matters seemed to present no mystery. One event occurred, however, during those early days, that did not so easily make sense. We came on the scene, it happened, a few weeks after the Bureau of Indian Affairs had first proposed to the Fox an action that seemed to me innocuous: they proposed to transfer the eighth grade from the local federally operated Fox school to the public junior high school in Tama. As the Fox put it, "the government is trying to take away the eighth grade from our school, make the kids go to Tama." One day in early summer Bureau officials traveled down from their regional headquarters in Minneapolis to get the Fox answer. The Fox seven-man tribal council met in formal session, with others of the tribe present according to their individual wishes. The proposal had a certain obvious logic and, in any event, seemed from the outside a matter of no very large importance. The Fox, however, reacted with great intensity. They said, "No," and they appeared angry and frightened.

The school matter dragged on several days, and in the end the government officials transferred the eighth grade without Fox consent. It was during those days that several Fox told me, as they had earlier told others, about the History, Fox history as seen by Fox men. The story focused on the land, those few Fox acres, the meaning of which seemed very important to them. The Fox had bought these Iowa acres. Fox beginnings were, said the tellers, too remote to explain easily, but for many generations they had lived in the vicinity of what is now Green Bay, Wisconsin. Then the Europeans came, and under the impact of displaced tribes from the east and of white settlers, the Fox had gradually displaced other tribes and had moved southward into southern Illinois and westward across the Mississippi into Iowa.

In the middle 1800's the History continued, the Black Hawk War had flared, involving mainly the Sac—a closely allied tribe who speak a dialect intelligible to the Fox—but also involving some of the Fox in open hostility with the United States Army. After the war many Fox had been removed by the federal government to a reservation in Kansas. Flat, treeless Kansas had been unpleasant, in part because of increased pressures to adopt new practices—pressures, as the History put it, "to build brick houses and become Christians" and to divide their tribal land into individually owned plots. So in 1854 the tribe had sent five or six leaders to their recent homelands in Iowa to find a place to live. These men were able to sell horses and buy eighty acres along the Iowa River and had obtained formal permission from the governor to settle there; there were papers somewhere, a treaty, that contained that agreement. The people on the Kansas reservation had then joined the group in Iowa a few at a time, as had other scattered Fox families who had not removed to Kansas. Now and again over the next fifty years, the tribe had been able, with money due them from early treaties, to buy more land. In buying the land, the History said, they had acquired a permanent home no longer vulnerable to the actions of white armies and others. They had bought the land collectively, and it was still owned by the tribal body. The land, the History concluded, will belong to their children and their children's children.

But there was more. That History, it soon became evident, was a secular version, told for the secular ears of one who knew that Paine and Washington, not God, sat down and made white America—*e pluribus unum* and all that. Fox History had, in addition, a sacred version, the same facts told differently, but told to a white stranger cautiously, tentatively, watchful of the reaction. This sacred History began in a mythical past when world and peoples came to be. One of those peoples, by this sacred story, was the Fox. And it was that enduring mythic entity, the Fox, which did all those historical things according to some imperfectly known preordained plan. Which makes the History read quite differently.

It was not, however, apparent just what this History, secular or sacred, had to do with transferring the eighth grade to the public schools in Tama. The angry and frightened reaction to the transfer remained a mystery. When a community of people do things, their collective actions usually have meanings, and when such a community is small those meanings are usually clear. Evidently such meanings were somehow couched in the History, but they eluded me.

Thus, the Fox presented during those first days an exterior that seemed in large measure rather neutral and usually seemed to make sense, but which also included appearances that puzzled. And through it all, the unusual reserve of the Indians seemed almost hostile—or possibly not hostile at all. My prevailing mood was vague discomfort.

We began to settle down. Buying groceries and getting the news took my wife and me and our fellows, as it took the Indians, to Tama. There we met men who responded to broad smiles with similar smiles. Conversations moved easily from pleasant inconsequentials to matters of mutual interest, and with some we soon felt the beginnings of friendship. One mutual interest was the Indians, and over the next several weeks I often found myself talking with these new acquaintances about the Indians. So without design or intent on my part, other outlines of Fox life began early to take shape in my mind—those outlines that existed in the minds of the white neighbors of the Fox.

The Fox presented, it seemed, a less puzzling exterior to their Tama County neighbors, to the white men for whom the Indians worked or from whom they bought groceries or with whom they sometimes drank in the white towns around. The Fox lived two miles from Tama, four miles from another town, eight miles from a third. Many Fox went to those towns several times a week. The Indians knew their white neighbors and had often known their fathers. These white Iowans knew the Fox and called them by name.

The Fox did not often engage in detailed conversation with these neighbors about happenings at home or in the Fox community, and it was a simple geographic fact that white neighbors were not likely to be present when most of the things occurred that together were Fox life—in Fox homes, for example, when families ate or visited. Of course, this spatial separation was equally true for the several neighboring white towns; the people of Tama saw almost as little of the people of Montour as they did of the Fox. But the people of Tama could read between the lines and from slight clues keep tabs on the less visible events in the homes in Montour. They seemed unable to read as easily or as completely between the lines from what they saw of the Indians.

Nevertheless these neighbors did not often express puzzlement over the visible events that unfolded among the Fox. The Fox reaction to the proposals of the Indian Bureau about the eighth grade was no surprise or mystery, it seemed. "The Fox," said the neighbors when I asked, "want the government to take care of them," and this accounted for the Fox reaction. Indeed, that Fox reaction seemed to those white neighbors fully predictable.

In general, the neighbors of the Fox thought quite often about the Indians, and if asked by a stranger they were usually willing to tell what they knew. Many of them seemed most comfortable, most sure of themselves, when they talked about first one and then another Fox individual. The same Fox names kept coming up, six or eight names in all. A Tama shopkeeper would say: "Pete Bear* is a good man, but he doesn't have too much influence out there any more." Or: "Tom Youngbird has a lot of influence out there, but you have to know how to handle him." Often there would follow some brief comments on the things that seemed to please and displease the named Fox, that is, some general outline of the man as his white neighbor imagined him to be, and almost always a statement as to whether that particular Fox was for or against "progress." Then, the speaker's mind would typically run to some past attempt on his part to get something done in the Indian community and he would tell of the diffi-

---

* All Indian names in this book are fictitious.

culties encountered and the part played by Bear or Youngbird.

I asked, in effect, "What is the Fox community like?" and I was told of a few influential Fox men. Fox life, that is, was often described by naming those individuals who appeared to have influence among the Indians and who appeared more or less "handleable" when their likes and dislikes were known. The minds of many of the white men of Tama seemed to run most comfortably in this direction, especially for those who had recent memories of trying to get something done for or with the Indians.

But other conversations ran in quite different directions. Often, the white neighbors of the Indians would tell what "the Fox," all of them taken together, were like. A farmer said, "Those Indians keep their word," and another said, "They're O.K. if you watch them." Indeed, one man might say both things within a few minutes. A woman said, "They're very spiritual, but rather unsanitary, you know." They're smart and they're dumb, they're courteous and rude, straightforward and shy, and so on, as individual Iowans remembered their experiences with individual Indians, generalized from those experiences, and reported on all the Fox.

By and large, these words—even the uncomplimentary ones —were spoken in kindness and with good intent. Most of the neighbors of the Fox seemed to feel some affection for the Indians. Their affection was abstract and distant, but there was little visible hostility. The portraits so drawn were various and often contradictory.

About certain matters, however, I found almost no diversity of opinion about the Fox; to me, a newcomer, the neighbors spoke as one man in expounding a kind of public line about the Indians. Within the first few minutes of conversation virtually every white Iowan advanced this line, and in repeated conversations it was never quite contradicted. The line was rarely accompanied by hostility, though it seemed to the tellers uncomplimentary. The usual opening was, "It's not all *their* fault, but . . ."

This public line about the Fox consisted of only three assertions, and these fitted one with the other. The first was: *"The Indians are unambitious nowadays; they're going to have to buck up out there."*

The Indians must "buck up," the neighbors said. What did the neighbors see that caused them to suppose that the typical Fox lacked ambition and needed to buck up? A relatively rare event, such as the Fox reaction over the eighth grade, evoked such descriptions. But further conversation usually revealed that the white men thought, when they said this, of more everyday matters, of what they had seen of the Fox on the job or of what the Fox had done and not done with Fox land. With much of Indian life hidden from sight, it was not surprising that impressions of Fox men and women at work should loom large. Fox working behavior was tangibly there for all to see, fifty-two weeks each year. No Fox family could live by the traditional devices of gardening, hunting, or gathering wild berries, and there was no special government dole that went out to them in monthly checks, so the Indians did the same kinds of work as their neighbors. A few Fox grew field corn on the Indian land for cash income; most traveled to factories in nearby towns and cities or worked with construction crews or railroad work crews out of those cities and towns. The corn on the Indian land was high or it was not; the Indian men drove by toward the factory at eight or they did not; you could measure it, if you wished, in dollar income per family per year. Here, then, was a very large part of the Fox public face.

Many of the neighbors knew the facts in greater detail. Iowa was rich farm land, but the 3,350 acres of the Indian settlement were not a good sample. The Indian river bottoms flooded; much of the land consisted of rough and wooded hills. Still, perhaps a third of the land would permit fairly intensive farming, but the Indians farmed it indifferently. White Iowans grew lush, ten-foot-high corn in hundred-acre plots, bought spindly calves and fed them the corn, and sold them later as prime beef; they fitted in other crops in complex rotation to restore soil nutrients, and as markets rose and fell sometimes other animals were fattened. These white men practiced a highly mechanized, tightfisted, hardheaded, intense, tightly scheduled, and (given government subsidy) a very profitable way of farming. White men in Iowa thus took wealth from nature, turned much of the wealth into machines, and turned the machines back against nature to extract more wealth.

But the Indians did not seem motivated in these directions. Few Indians were farmers of cash crops, and even they did not appear very serious about it and did not depend on the land for all their living. The white men in Iowa wondered: 3,350 acres and not a cow on them! They had difficulty understanding this kind of behavior toward the land. The Indians did not act like Iowa farmers, and they did not seem to think like Iowa farmers. The neighbors of the Fox left it at that, and did not like it.

Similarly, in the factories and on construction crews white men saw the Indians day in and day out. No one said the Fox did not "put out"; they were known to work very hard. But fellow workers heard about other things: a Fox was getting into his car to leave his house for work when his uncle walked up, and they talked about the weather; the uncle mentioned casually that he thought he might go to Marshalltown if he could get a ride; nephew and uncle got in the car and went not to work, but to Marshalltown.

Perhaps because of this behavior, many Fox—about half the work force—had come to find themselves in the unskilled jobs often filled by white semi-vagrants: railroad repair work, seasonal construction work. An equal number of Fox men had gone into more steady and skilled jobs, had become welders, tool operators, and the like. The whites were aware of and told about these "good workers" but held them to be exceptions. A third kind of Fox worker seemed remarkable by his total absence: no Fox quite resembled the driving would-be member of the middle class, working hard and saving, striving for wealth and status. Of course, this third kind of behavior was the ideal in the minds of most of white Iowa.

Thus, the neighbors saw Indian workers they deemed undependable, hence inadequate except for unskilled, irregular work. They saw other Indians, about equal in number, who had come to adequate terms with the American economy, but these seemed to leave less forceful impressions. They saw no driving "middle class" Indians. And they saw those untidy Fox corn fields. "The Fox," they said inclusively, "are unambitious and must buck up, make something of themselves." During the early weeks of my stay in the Indian community, I fell often into easy conversation with many of the white men of Tama: shopkeepers, farmers, housewives, teachers, clerks, and occasionally (too rarely) common laborers and drifters. Most told me this; none quite contradicted it.

A second aspect of visible Fox life was noted and described by the neighbors as with one voice: *The Indians are too dependent; the government takes care of everything out there because the Indians won't.* And some would add, ". . . and we pay the taxes." Within the first ten minutes of almost every conversation about the Fox, this was mentioned.

As before, a rare event might evoke this description of Fox life, but in the main it was everyday matters that these neighbors had in mind. What they had observed was real enough, as they easily pointed out. They failed to see anything in Fox life analogous to the busy affairs that demanded the energies of their own self-governing small towns. When a Tama citizen encountered a man from nearby Toledo, they could chat about shared problems in getting their respective school boards to establish a consolidated high school, or getting a paving bill through their councils. When this same man from Tama met an Indian, there was no such common experience. Nor could men from Tama often observe Indians talking to other Indians about such matters; instead, they told about Fox leaders, tribal councilmen, who seemed to fear to act and who when they acted often were not followed. Instead of seeing Indians busying themselves over their community affairs, white men of Tama County saw the conspicuous presence of white federal administrators going in and out of town about Indian business, present for the sole purpose of taking care of the Fox.

The Fox grade school, for example, was run, from the principal to the janitor, by federal employees who were not legally responsible to anyone within the Indian community they served. The tribal council could legally initiate only the most routine actions. The Bureau of Indian Affairs could and often did initiate action to be put into effect whether the Indians approved or not—often against their express wishes, as every neighbor had at some time observed and could recount. The tribal council, in short, was revealed to the white neighbors as impotent, and by extension that was what the Fox as individuals and as a community seemed to be. In the *de facto* relationship between the Fox and the federal officials the Indians attempted to get the best they could from others who held the power; they wheedled and dickered, but they did not govern.

This, it appeared, was not a matter that depended much on the personalities of particular officials of the Bureau of Indian

Affairs. Officials had come and gone over the years; the manner of running Fox affairs had changed hardly at all. Bureau officials were by law responsible for the minutiae of, say, school affairs; should money be misspent, the officials were legally responsible. The whole bureaucracy was organized to handle, through a chain of command, that legal responsibility.

As the neighbors described it, the government was there taking care of education and health; earlier they had taken care of roads and law enforcement, but responsibility for these services had recently been turned over to the neighbors of the Fox. What the neighbors usually inferred was that the government had to take care of these things because the Fox could not. There, visibly, were the federal servants, going about their work (and doing their impossible job well, by and large). To the neighbors of the Fox this was unmistakable, and one of the more salient facts about the Fox community.

The whites consistently said a third thing about the Fox, but I was harder put to learn what of Fox life was visibly seen to cause the notion. They said: *"When the Indian kids grow up, you won't find them hanging around out there; they're getting an education and then they'll get away."* These neighbors were saying that the Fox as a community were temporary.

When white Iowans said that the Fox were unambitious or that they were dependent, they pointed to visible Fox actions from which those inferences could with some reason be drawn. Here they did not. Conversations revealed that some Fox individuals did leave the community, and their names were remembered by their neighbors; they went to Des Moines, or St. Louis, or Chicago, and sometimes (but not usually) they cut their ties and their children became strangers to the community. But this had been going on for a long time, at least two generations, and during that time the population of the community had doubled. This, too, many neighbors knew. Virtually all adult Fox, except a few of the oldest, were literate and had work skills and they stayed; it was not clear that the children now in school were learning other things to make larger numbers of them do differently. It was not even clear why those few then in colleges would necessarily live great distances away or would necessarily divorce themselves from their friends and family.

Less than one hundred miles from the Fox were the Amanas, a wealthy colony founded by German pietists. Conversations did not reveal that the men of Tama felt that the Amanas were a temporary community, or that they should have been (though they did often suggest ways the Amanas had changed or ought to change). Yet to these same Iowans it seemed improbable that the Indians would remain a community for more than, as they put it, another generation.

Perhaps the neighbors were expressing a kind of hope for the Fox. Earlier they had said the Fox were a people who seemed unambitious and who were dependent on the government. These two notions together were perhaps less than tolerable to Iowa farmers and businessmen. Probably such behavior seemed to impose an unreasonable demand on their pocketbooks. Probably, too, it seemed to them a denial of some condition of human decency they felt the Fox deserved or should have. So they predicted that it would all go away, that the Fox as a community would disappear.

Conversations, then, with our new white acquaintances in Tama shortly revealed these gross outlines of Fox life. The pictures were of course incomplete: I was not by these outlines helped to visualize what happened inside Fox homes. Also, the white men of Tama sometimes mentioned in passing sundry other things that had no apparent connection. They sometimes mentioned "the Indian religion," but what had been said about apparent lack of ambition did not permit me to imagine what a Fox god might be like, and the neighbors did not seem to know. Or they mentioned "Indian games," but I could not envisage how a dependent people might play.

Nevertheless, that part of the description which was asserted alike by all the white men, the public line about the Indians, had a kind of internal logic and, by the virtual unanimity with which it was told, one might assume that the white men found it unusually compelling and satisfying. The line did in fact account in a rough way for yesterday's Fox behavior and predict tomorrow's, to the satisfaction of the neighbors of the Fox. White Iowans did not seem to find the Indians puzzling.

We began living among the Fox and their neighbors in early July, 1952; at the end of the summer my two fellow students returned to Chicago according to plan, while my wife and I remained. In the early fall I went briefly to Chicago, "for consultations," as it was generously phrased. Actually, the trip was for intellectual help and moral support. That initial question, what can you see if you look? was still there. It still evoked anxiety. And everything that had occurred over the summer—all those conversations with the Fox and with their neighbors—all this had only increased my anxiety.

I was able, in Chicago, to sketch out the assertions made about the Fox by the white men—the Fox are unambitious and dependent and (therefore) the community is temporary —and the one assertion made by the Fox about themselves— the Fox intend to be permanent (or in the sacred version, more simply, the Fox *are*). It was embarrassingly little to show.

These assertions had no evident value as descriptions of Fox life. But the assertions themselves were facts, social facts, verbal baggage of some sort, carried in the heads of the

Indians and their neighbors and in some way entering and affecting their frequent encounters. In Chicago I discussed that problem a bit with my teachers and fellow students, and then we turned to sundry matters of finance, equipment, and so on.

I returned to the Fox to ponder, not much comforted. One thing had become clear: whatever I had hold of, it was not a verbal argument between the Fox and their neighbors. The Fox told me the History and did not, so far as I could see, talk much about it with their neighbors. Similarly the white men gave me, not the Fox, their public line. Between the Fox and their neighbors there was action and reaction, not talk. Yet they told me those few things, not countless other thinkable things, and they told them in the midst of their actions and reactions. Their words had, surely, some connection with their actions. That was the question: what connection?

The dramatic encounter with the Bureau of Indian Affairs over the eighth grade, simply because it was dramatic, provided in retrospect a clue. It then became apparent: the proposed change in the school had been seen by the Indians as part of some larger invitation extended to the Fox, an invitation to disappear. The language used by the government frequently included words like "progress" and "integration." In addition, the proposed change had come from the government in the form of impending unilateral action (soon carried through); perhaps that very threat had suggested to the Indians that the government officials already supposed that the Fox had ceased to exist effectively, as a historic community with enduring relations with the federal government based on real historic events, relations mutually binding. Individual Indians had varied in the intensity of their resistance to the eighth grade proposal, but the resistance had come very close to being categorical—so close that, for all public thoughts and acts, Fox resistance had been unqualified. To the government officials the Indians spoke vaguely of past treaties. To me they recounted the History.

The Indians, we heard at the time from harried officials of the Bureau, had in recent years instantly opposed other suggested changes—in their school system, in their trust status, in the jurisdiction of their law and order. They had seemed opposed to the very idea of change, irrespective of the substantive details, which never were much discussed.

The neighbors of the Fox had, of course, observed all this or heard about it. There, as they saw it, were the Indians perpetually resisting change, forever poised against the government and its reasonable proposals. The neighbors noted the blanket resistance and they put their usual construction on it. They saw it as further evidence that the Fox indeed were woefully unambitious and were indeed chronically dependent. But, they added, that would go away in another generation. Indian resistance in the affair over the eighth grade had, in fact, evoked just such a white response. To the Indians they talked of education. But to me, the neighbors of the Fox kept telling their public line about the Indians.

Dramatic encounters provided the clue, but everyday realities resided in everyday affairs, in this instance in the daily encounters between individual Indians and their individual white neighbors on the streets of Tama. When a white man chanced to meet an individual Fox, what mind-set might he have brought to that encounter? It seemed possible that this public line created for that white man a clear mind-set of wide utility and of some power, so that whatever additional bits he might see of Fox life could be "handled"—could be interpreted, put in meaningful place, be made publicly meaningful.

The Fox were seen as unambitious, dependent, and temporary. Thus the mind-set: is this individual Fox, from what he has just said or done, heading up and out? or is he not? Is he moving toward things white? or is he staying with that distressing and dying thing, the Fox community?

With some frequency I heard white comments about this or that Indian who practiced the "Indian religion" (which seemed to the teller unfortunate), or who indulged in "Indian games" (which seemed to the teller rather childish), or about "progressive" Indians (who were good) or other Indians who "went back" (who were, in this respect, not good). And so on. Thus it appeared that the neighbors of the Fox shared among themselves a roughly coherent set of evaluations that in the rush of everyday affairs would, with some consistency, rank individual Fox men and their actions in an order from bad to good: men were Fox-like and not good, or white-like and better, and the very best were the ones who left. (And through all this, the neighbors told me, not the Indians, their public line about the Fox.)

Conversely, when an individual Fox chanced to meet one of his white neighbors, what mind-set might he have brought to that encounter? One could suppose that almost no casual encounter on the streets of Tama failed to express to the Fox in a host of unsubtle cues, a gracious invitation to (as the Fox would view it) a kind of social death. Most Fox, as they had resisted the Bureau's invitation to disappear, would resist or evade or withdraw from these everyday invitations to cease, as a community, to be. (And through all this, the Fox told me, not their neighbors, the History.)

A circle seemed joined. The visible face of the Indian community was interpreted by their neighbors to reveal lack of ambition and lack of independence, which seemed so unattractive as to cause the neighbors to hope for the early absorption of the Fox community into the general population; thus the neighbors acted consciously and otherwise, to encourage and assist that transition. But the Fox, by virtue of their very different image of their past and future, resisted any changes that seemed to imply the end of their community. In turn, the publicly visible Fox resistance underscored and reinforced in the minds of their neighbors the original image of an unambitious, dependent people.

Such seemed to have been the enduring core of the relations between these Indians and their neighbors. These relations were at an impasse. It was an impasse unintended and, as a total system, unrecognized. There was no violence, and there was some kindness and abstract affection and much good intent. But these relations were not enjoyable, nor relaxed. The neighbors of the Fox were estranged from the Fox.

I was in the Fox community to do something called "action anthropology," to help while learning and to learn while helping. It seemed I had stumbled upon a bizarre word game: critically, the white men saw an array of Fox behavior and (unknown to the Fox) called it "lack of ambition" and "dependency" and inferred that the Fox were temporary, while the Fox looked back upon their past and forward to their future and (unknown to their neighbors) called it the History. From these two constructions, it seemed, the whole circle of cause and effect was daily created and recreated.

I was, thus, on the fringes of that bizarre word game, and I decided to join it, to play; I took sides with the Indians. To play seemed, as the saying goes, like a good idea at the time.

To begin with, I wrote a couple of pamphlets and a long series of articles for the *Tama News-Herald*; all were attempts to examine rhetorically such matters as lack of ambition, dependency, the permanence or impermanence of the Fox community, and other matters less central. My aim was to redefine the visible Fox behavior that so disturbed the whites, using words that would make the behavior seem more congenial. The effects, of course, were zero: those white men's words simply would not go away. Evidently, those white minds were in the firm grip of habits of mind, perhaps created and daily recreated by those words. Such matters one cannot affect with rhetoric.

In short, perhaps by a tyranny of words still mysterious, the neighbors of the Fox were estranged from the Fox. It should be noted, though it must be evident, so was the writer.

3. First Studies

"THE INDIANS," said the neighbors of the Fox, "are unambitious and dependent." "The Zuni," Ruth Benedict had said much earlier in *Patterns of Culture*, "are Apollonian." The similarity is clear enough: both were looking at a human community and both were describing that community by describing a typical kind of man, letting the characteristic behavior of one imaginary man stand for the community.

It appeared, however, that the neighbors of the Fox, describing in that fashion, had estranged themselves from the Fox; Ruth Benedict, on the other hand, had not seemed estranged from the Zuni. What then, was the underlying difference? To me, a very raw student of anthropology, that was not an idle question.

A gross answer suggested itself, which in turn, during the fall months of 1952, launched a series of brief inquiries about the Fox that might in some generosity be called studies of the Fox community.

The gross difference was this. The neighbors of the Fox, it seemed in retrospect, had not actually reported on what the Fox were, but on what they were not. It was as if the whites had gone to the Fox with a check list of behavior, the real or imagined behavior of white Iowans, and had measured the Fox against it. By these standards, the typical Fox might very well not behave ambitiously (as white Iowans measure ambition), not behave independently, not behave in a lot of ways.

Ruth Benedict, in apparent contrast, had gone to the Zuni, had immersed herself in Zuni life (vicariously, in large measure), had more or less successfully kept such a list out of hand and out of mind, and had discerned inductively from the ebb and flow of Zuni life some salient and characteristic behavior of a Zuni kind of man.

The neighbors of the Fox partially described one kind of man the Fox were not. Benedict partially described the kind of men the Zuni were. I began, that fall of 1952, to imitate Ruth Benedict, in a very primitive way.

The life of the Fox had gone on; I had begun to get a dim sense of where one could in common decency intrude and where not; a first acquaintance among the people had led to a second and these to invitations into a house or to a ritual feast. A good deal of community life was thus being paraded. I watched and listened, guided by one preoccupying mode of looking and thinking. Describing Fox life in imitation of Benedict's work seemed to me attractive: of the things that went on in the community, I began to see much that appeared to be characteristic of the Fox kind of man.

The first events of Fox life that became reasonably clear

were those seeming to express recurrent consistencies of behavior. Of all such events, the most revealing were those where
outsiders were not much involved: informal Indian dancing
at the Pow-wow grounds; a Fox funeral and the formal
adoption rituals that followed some weeks after in which
surviving children adopted a ceremonial parent; and several
others. All these events were people doing things togther that
required the coordination of individual efforts. Such co-
ordination, it was evident, was made easier by the fact that
the men so thrown together acted in certain consistent ways.
It became apparent that, generally in such events, the Fox
were conspicuously generous, and unusually circumspect and
unassuming toward each other. These were, it appeared, two
characteristic behaviors of the Fox kind of man.

The typical Fox is generous. Out of the welter of everyday
events, earlier events as they were recalled to mind and other
events as they unfolded, an impression emerged that, in some
frequency that would appear noteworthy to men not Fox (at
least to *some* kinds of non-Fox), these Indians gave things
to each other. I talked to Indians, also, about Fox events I
had not yet myself seen. A pattern emerged. In the event of
a death, a great many families gave food or money to the
bereaved family. In the event of any one of several kinds of
ceremonial feast, some men brought food and other men
partook of the ceremonial meal. Altogether these ceremonial
events (funerals, ceremonial adoption, calendrical religious
feasts, and others) might occur some twenty-odd times in a
year. The list of ritualized and institutionalized giving could
be extended.

The Fox kind of man is generous. In a very approximate
way this assertion did sum up much that went on in Fox life.
It was of course also true that the typical Fox was typically
not generous; in all the instances suggested, some Fox gave

while others received and still others were simply uninvolved; or a certain man might give in one context and not give in another; and on many kinds of Fox occasions, no one gave anything to anyone. More accurately, then, I should have said, "The Fox kind of man is (and is not) generous," which was not a very satisfying thing to know about the Fox. So I fell back to the more satisfying, if misleading, assertion: the Fox kind of man is generous.

Yet the mere frequency of occasion for generosity did affect the operation and shape of the Fox economy, did cause goods to flow in ways they otherwise would not. The community was economically poor; annual cash income was between $1,000 and $2,000 per family. Primarily, the Indians were laborers; there were about 150 workers in the community of whom only about 70 per cent would be employed, part time or full time, at any given time of the year. There were other minor sources of income. The income from a tribal fund, Fox money that remained from a settlement at the time of some remote treaty and that was held for the tribe in the United States Treasury, was distributed to some Fox, generally children, semiannually; payments were about five dollars per person. The annual Fox Pow-wow, held in August each year for white paying guests, was a celebration at least as much as it was an economic effort, but it did present an opportunity for some Fox to earn twenty-five to thirty dollars once a year by taking part in the dancing or in other work. Many Indian families also derived a bit income from beaded souvenir items, but the time required for manufacture was out of all proportion to the money the articles brought.

The Fox were poor, but they talked very little about their poverty. The more drastic effects of low income were lessened by three facts peculiar to the Indian community. Most of the Indians were relatively indifferent to some of the material needs that require a large share of the income of the average white family. A Fox house was a shelter and in no part a status marker. Second, no Fox ever had personal expenses in connection with his home site; there was no rent or mortgage and the tribe paid the taxes on all the tribal land by income earned from leasing a small part of it to a white farmer. The third fact was a direct effect of Fox generosity: on crisis occasions the Fox gave. This custom made it unnecessary for an individual to lay up a nest egg in anticipation of the next crisis; if there were a death, the Indians gave a bit of money to the family, or if a man were temporarily out of a job his relatives and others close to him usually gave him food. These forms of mutual assistance in crisis added up to a sort of insurance system. The community was very poor, but the poverty did not seem to grind.

Fox generosity affected the shape of the Fox economy in at least one other way. It virtually guaranteed, for example, that a man would not prosper as a storekeeper: how deny help when all the needed food was tangibly there on the shelves? There were few Fox entrepreneurs and none of them was well off.

Perhaps, then, it could be grossly said, and to some good descriptive purpose, that a typical Fox is generous.

Similarly: *The typical Fox is circumspect.* In their relations with each other the Fox gave the appearance of a gentle, unassuming people. This was observable in virtually all contexts.

I had early sensed a certain discomfort among Fox men in positions of apparent authority, i.e., as members of the Fox tribal council. It seemed possible that these, and Fox men generally, were reluctant to move into positions where they seemed to be above their fellows, instructing them or deciding matters for them. Walter Miller, a fellow student of anthropology, had worked among the Fox in the summers of 1948 and 1949; he studied Fox political organization and wrote a remarkable report on the manner in which the Fox exercised authority in most forms. A host of confirming examples soon forced themselves upon me.

I shall quote Miller at some length. He writes in *Documentary History of the Fox Project:*

> Were you to visit the present day Fox settlement during the bright warm days of late August, you would find yourself in the midst of a colorful and impressive exhibition of organized activity. This is the "Pow-wow," a four day public celebration put on each year by the Fox. You would see Indians directing traffic, ushering and seating a large crowd of white visitors, collecting admission, selling souvenirs, staging a program of native music and dances. You would realize that this was an enterprise that required the co-ordination of considerable numbers of people; detailed advanced planning; arrangements as to publicity and accommodations; collection and disbursement of funds. It would seem evident that the direction of this enterprise lay in the hands of an efficient and well organized administrative body; a group capable of initiating a complex enterprise and exercising the authority necessary to see it through successfully. . . .
>
> The Pow-wow is the outstanding example of successfully co-ordinated group action, and thus of effective co-ordinative authority in Fox society today. By Fox standards it is a large-scale enterprise—semi-commercial, semi-ritualized in nature—that involves the participation of almost every member of the tribe. The Pow-wow has been functioning, in some form or other, for at least seventy-five years; it has maintained a formal adminis-

trative organization for 39 years. It is evident that in the reasons for the success of this enterprise we can find important clues to the problem of effective authority in Fox society.

The Pow-wow was a natural and gradual outgrowth of the traditional Fox religious rituals. . . . Shortly after the arrival in Iowa of the Tama Fox, newspapers reported that local whites had been invited to witness the songs and dances that made up the traditional Fox four-day harvest ceremonies—held each year during the latter part of August. An 1879 account states that "quite a number of people of Tama were present to witness the ceremonies . . . of the annual Pow-wow." In these early days a few bales of hay were set up as seats for whites to witness what was essentially a secularized religious ceremony. As the years passed increasing white attendance prompted the addition of non-religious events such as horse-racing and games to what were then called the annual "field days," but the administration of the event was essentially that of the religious ceremonial. . . .

Today the Pow-wow is under the direction of the all-Indian Pow-wow committee. The committee consists of 16 positions—four staff and twelve line. Elections for committee membership are held every two years with the total tribe electorate taking part in the voting. Theoretically all positions are open at each election, but in practice there is a remarkable degree of overlap from year to year. Four of the 1951 committee members were also on the 1925 committee—some having served continuously. Committee membership lists show that there is, in effect, a "spot" on the committee for a representative of each important family group, and the selection of committee members from year to year tends to follow the pattern of having each family represented on each committee. Thus, while recruitment of committee members is theoretically by "free" popular election, in actuality the traditional Fox pattern of all-family-group representation in authority organs strongly influences the choice of members.

The four staff offices are President, Vice-president, Secretary, and Treasurer. Of these, the nominally para-mount authority-role, that of President, carries with it vitually no real authority. The President is almost always either an elderly man, or someone who maintains a high degree of interest in the old traditions and dances. He has very little to do either with the actual direction of the Pow-wow, or with technical arrangements. The most "important" of the staff positions is that of Secretary. Most of the authority functions of the secretary involve contacts with whites outside the settlement—arrangements as to publicity, procurement, transportation, special events, and the like—so the person selected for this role is almost always a young man, educated and reasonably competent in the ways of the whites. He must be acquainted with white business and commercial practices, and be able to "deal with the whites." However, his authority functions are almost purely "liaison" functions, and he has very little to say about the direction and co-ordination of the tribal participants in the Pow-wow itself.

How, then *is* this enterprise co-ordinated? Co-ordination is effected very largely by the adherence of participants to traditionally established and well known procedures. It is remarkable to observe how an enterprise the size of the Pow-wow, with a fairly complex and ramified division of labor, is co-ordinated with so small an amount of overt authority exercise. People know their jobs and do them. If you ask someone how he knows what to do without having someone tell him, he will say, "I just do the same thing as I did last year." This is possible because there are few changes from year to year. There is very little centralization of or control over concessions. At the 1951 Pow-wow there were 24 separate souvenir stands, each run by a different family group. No attempt is made to consolidate these in the interests of increased "efficiency." Any [Fox] who wishes can set up a stand or booth without the necessity of committee approval.

Thus the Pow-wow committee, as an authority organ, exercises few directive functions. It has two main functions. First, it is a "consensus group," a representative body that handles whatever decision-making is necessary by the traditional process of long discussion and unanimous consent. Its meetings are open to all the tribe, and the majority of its decisions are unanimous. It is not an "innovating" body; most of its decisions deal with relatively minor aspects of established practices, and there is a decided resistance to the acceptance of "new" practices. Being quite large in proportion to the size of the total enterprise, and broadly representative, the committee is very sensitive and responsive to the wishes of all the people in the matters it deals with.

Secondly, the committee is a work-gang; staff members are a reasonably dependable agency for the performance of the manual labor involved in staging the Pow-wow—erecting tents and tipis; putting up the benches; filling in ruts and hollows; cleaning the area. Very little of this work is delegated. Committeemen, along with all tribal participants are paid for their services according to the number of work-hours they put in, with the same hourly rate prevailing for all tribal members. Service on the committee carries with it the prestige of community service; "It takes up a lot of time," says one committeeman, "but it's fun, working for the good of the people."

It is important to note at this point the extent to which the conduct of the Pow-wow follows traditional Fox practices, while maintaining the formal organization of the American association." *

Thus I was given a glimpse of how the Fox handled authority, as it worked itself out in the recurrent task of staging the annual Pow-wow. The Pow-wow was, of course, a show for profit; the Fox did make some money during the afternoon and evening performances. But they also kept on dancing and visiting their Indian guests and one another around the campfires most nights until four and five A.M.; the Pow-wow was more than a show. Through the Pow-wow perhaps, the Fox gave themselves an occasion to announce to an audience and to themselves, "We are Fox Indians," and to enact and express and thereby believe that fact. In this letter, I judged, lay the main source of the popular commitment, which was altogether essential if such a large and complex undertaking was to be organized by a people who refused to boss or be bossed.

Miller's full report considers the whole range of occasions when Fox men needed to coordinate their activities politically. Again and again he reports how very gingerly the Fox handled

* Excerpts from Fred Gearing, Robert McC. Netting, Lisa R. Peattie, eds. (Department of Anthropology, The University of Chicago, copyright by The University of Chicago, 1960), pp. 127-146.

authority. Most dramatically, perhaps, in political discussion: meetings continued until unanimity was reached, and if that were impossible the matter would usually be left undecided.

To me, as to Miller, the strong Fox sense that a Fox is circumspect was visible in almost every situation. In conversation Fox eyes rarely met, and Fox spoke in a low voice. In formal and informal discussions sentiments were expressed with "They say . . . ," not "I believe . . . ." And if others disagreed, their expressed sentiments were countered not directly but by cautious implication. Fox avoided appearing to stare at another, say, who passed down the road. Fox stringently avoided open argument or violence with fellow Fox, failing in this only under severe provocation or when they were drunk. Similarly, in their jobs a few Fox were foremen and the like, but not comfortably or very effectively when their crews were made up of other Fox. In those forms of organization where formal positions of leadership were required (as for the Pow-wows), the men who were elevated to these positions typically were able to exercise unusual caution so as not to appear to direct; even so, their lives were difficult.

It became possible to say that, in a remarkably pervading sense, the Fox kind of man is circumspect. A great deal of community life was summed up by this assertion. Exceptions existed, occasions when bluster or domination were decently possible, as in disciplining children, for example, or in certain historical behavior of warriors toward their fellows. But the exceptions were rare. I had hit upon a recurrent fact of Fox life; it was unusually illuminating, because Fox life happened to be in this respect unusually consistent.

A Fox kind of man is circumspect and, as we saw, generous. In our naming of those two recurrent patterns of behavior of the typical Fox, much of the welter of going and coming that was Fox life seemed to have been held still to the senses, to have come to be in some approximate sense described.

One additional feature of the Fox kind of man came into focus during these early inquiries: it consisted of a certain pattern of ideas of such a man, Fox ideas about the nature of things.

History, as the Fox told it, intruded. The History, in its sacred version, told about an enduring entity, the Fox, which came to be when most other human things came to be, a categorical "thing." The History told of another "thing," very closely related, the land. That reiterated History kept insisting on the importance of the land, and mainly by these reminders I became aware that I had begun to accumulate bits of information concerning Fox notions about the natural world generally, and I therefore sought more. I came to learn through Fox word and deed about their traditional view of the world of nature, "Fox natural science," if you will.

Fox land was, of course, to the Fox what home is to every man, the space that contained the known and familiar. Children grew up here; this was the place the people knew. They knew each small frame house and who lived there; they knew the spots in the river that were good for fishing and the woods that were good for squirrel; they knew the cemeteries; they knew the Pow-wow grounds, which were shady and quiet except in August of each year, when they erupted into color and activity; and so on. As home, the land was a set of landmarks each of which was invested with memories, good and bad; these acres were seen by the Fox in great detail, and they evoked affection.

The Fox thought about the land in a second way, a way that reflected Fox perceptions of the world of nature. A generation ago parts of the Fox land had been laid out by government workers in the precise rectangular manner of Iowa farms. The fences were still there and much of the same land was still plowed. But a geographer, William L. Thomas, once examined an aerial photograph of that section of Iowa and was able to do what seemed to me a very remarkable thing. With no knowledge to draw on other than the configuration of land and vegetation as revealed in that photo, Thomas was able to trace the approximate boundary of the Fox land. In some part this was easy: the idle and wooded land was Fox. But Thomas could also distinguish between a Fox farm and an adjoining white farm, devoted to the same cash crops. Compared to the sharply geometric precision around them, Thomas pointed out, Fox fence rows had over the years become a bit uneven and a little wider and the corners of the fields had become somewhat rounded. The Fox, even those who farmed for cash, did not appear particularly intent on holding the land in check.

These were but symptoms. Two generations ago, a thoughtful observer would have had little difficulty understanding the Indians' notions about the nature of the land. He would have found a Fox tradition, handed down by word of mouth, which explicity set forth such notions. That tradition would have asserted how the universe was formed, its ongoing nature, and the place of the Fox as a people in the natural order. That order would have been set forth as a balanced harmony of parts: land and its animals and vegetation, the sky, the Fox, numerous supernatural forces, and many other parts joined in a cosmic equilibrium enduring since the beginning. The tradition would also have told about the implied burdens borne by each Fox generation, the ways the Fox had necessarily to think and act in ritual and in more ordinary affairs to maintain the natural order of things.

A Fox Indian, then, would not have heard, as white men do, about one's moral obligation to subdue and exploit nature; he would have heard about an order that bound together nature and the Fox people in reciprocal necessity, one to the other. The hunter had of necessity to apologize to the hunted bear, for example, so as not to offend, and to insure that there would be hunters and bears the next year. The old men, two generations back, would have laid out those truths in the stories told the children through the long winter evenings, called, for this reason, the Winter Stories. An annual series of rituals would have expressed those truths through more compelling symbolic reference and insisted on them by means of the even greater compulsion of song and dance, rhythms of sound and motion moving to necessary rest.

The natural order was not static. Through the years, according to tradition, individual Fox men had, by fasting and other self-mortification, caused supernatural forces to "pity" them and thereby give them special gifts or "blessings," each of which established some slightly new relationship with some part of the natural order; and typically the blessings included some new ritual of song and dance which, if performed regularly, transmitted the blessings to succeeding Fox generations. So the Fox position in the natural order was not quite unchanging: it was a *modus operandi* cumulative through the generations and requiring of each generation specific acts if the order were to be maintained.

One such blessing, according to tradition, was anciently received from the buffaloes by a young man, and it is maintained through the "Buffalo head" ritual of one Fox kin group. In the 1920s Truman Michelson of the U.S. Bureau of American Ethnology collected and translated Fox accounts of the ritual and its origin. We may read in *Notes on The Buffalo-Head Dance of the Thunder Gens of the Fox Indians*, the translated words of a Fox:

Well, it seems a certain person soon began to have himself fast all winter as he desired to easily slay his enemies. Well, it seems that he continued to fast for four years. . . . Soon, it appears, while he slept he was summoned: "Come, you are summoned," he was told by someone as he was summoned. As soon as he was led some place, lo! there were many buffaloes. "Well," he was told, "ahead is from where we summon you," he was told. When he started to enter where a long wickiup was, lo! there was an old man, a human being, indeed, seated there. Yet it is a fact it was that buffalo. "Well, my grandchild, I take pity upon you as I am entirely too much grieved at your extreme wailing and weeping," he was told. "I take pity upon you," he was told, "but this is the way you will be: Even as far off as old age; to that extent shall I take compassion upon you. Now you must tell those of the one (kin group) to which you belong who shall live in the future, that whosoever shall earnestly think of you under future life shall be blessed by the way I take compassion upon you, my grandchild.

"And this: At the time when the manitou shall renew this earth of his, this (religion) will go and be there. Verily, if (any of) you shall properly carry it on somewhere, at that time you will again exist as mortals; if the people are remade you (may be) confident (that) you will again exist as mortals," it is said is what he was told.

"And this is what you shall ask for, this single slice. Also if you conduct (this religion) uprightly and well, you shall also be able to easily slay your foe," he was told. "And you, to be sure, will go to war twice, and twice you shall slay (foes)," he was told.

"And of those who shall exist as mortals in the distant time, whosoever shall continue to think of, and whosoever shall continue to earnestly remember this, the manner in which I bless you, shall forever live in health, always." That, it seems is what he was told . . . .

Then the young Fox was taken before other supernatural powers who confirmed the blessing. Finally he was told the ritual that would achieve the continued blessing.

"Now, my grandchild, now I shall tell you how I bless you. Suppose you were to think, 'how, pray, may it be that I shall be (rightly) understood if I worship?' Why this is how you will be able to make us understand: (it will be) at the time when you offer us this tobacco in earnest. This Spirit of Fire, verily, will be the first to gladly (receive it.) He is the one who will tell it again and again for you (who are) here with his breath the entire extent of this sky. So you speak to him whenever you remember us. And this one, your grandfather Who-lies-peeping-through-the smoke-hole, he also will tell it for you whenever you worship in any way. These are the only ones to whom you shall speak." . . .

So, annually, the ritual occurred, "Spirit of Fire" and "Who-lies-peeping-through-the-smoke-hole" acting as messengers to the other supernatural powers who, hearing, renewed the blessing. The ritual contained a series of songs and dances, then a ceremonial feast. Before the latter, when all who would eat had their food before them, the ceremonial leader spoke in formalistic language:

"Those (foods) are what we hand the manitou who are seated about us. The one who is in the east, so be it, at the end of the earth, so be it, is the one to whom we first hand these foods, so be it. Life, so be it, is what we collectively desire of him, so be it. Then again, so be it, the one who is yonder, so be it, at the end of the earth, so be it, toward the south, so be it, is also one whom we worship, so be it. We, so be it, also, so be it, ask, so be it, life, so be it, from him, so be it. Then again, so be it, the one who is yonder, so be it, toward the west, so be it, at the end of the earth, so be it, is also one whom we worship, so be it. We, so be it, also, so be it, ask, so be it, life from him, so be it. Then again, so be it, that is why we collectively worship, so be it, the one who is in the north, so be it, so that he will bless us the same way. That, so be it, is what we ask of him, so be it. For this reason, so be it, you may eat, so be it, women, and also men. Eat!" They said, "Very well," and began to eat . . . .

Then followed more dancing, imitative of the buffaloes, accompanied by the following song:

A clean buffalo spoke to me;
    (Repeat)
A clean buffalo spoke to me, spoke to me;
A clean buffalo spoke to me;
    (Repeat twice)

The southern buffalo spoke to you;
    (Repeat six times)
The southern buffalo spoke to you, spoke to you.

They have left me standing there;
Wherever you may go;
> (Repeat twice)

What is it?
> (Repeat seven times)

This buffalo who stands upon this earth;
What is it?
> (Repeat five times)

They have left me standing there;
> (Repeat six times)

Why, he, that buffalo, is my friend, my friend;
> (Repeat)

Here upon this earth; my friend; my friend; my friend;
Why, he is my friend;
Why he is my friend, my friend.*

In this vein the ritual continued from morning until late afternoon, a reiteration of one facet of the cosmic order that bound the Fox and nature in a set of obligations each to the other.

Two generations back an outsider might readily have recognized such a view of the world in Fox word and deed. In this generation the Winter Stories seemed to be told less often, and only to some Fox children.

In 1952 the annual round of rituals still went on, including the Buffalo head ceremony. But the Indians could no longer accept their truth as self-evident, without reflection, because

* Smithsonian Institution, Bureau of American Ethnology, Bulletin 87 (U.S. G.P.O., 1928), pp. 43-75.

millions all around denied that truth; many Fox believed, but many were skeptical, and a few claimed disbelief. Yet a basic sense about the nature of the land seemed to persist. I said previously that the Fox exploited the land poorly. That English sentence misled; the Fox did not "expolit" the land at all. These Indians seemed rather to imagine themselves living with the land in preordained harmony, even though the mythic rationale was no longer frequently expressed and appeared to be less precise in the minds of many.

One fall day I chanced to drive through the Iowa country-side, the landscape wrought by white Iowa farmers: rolling hills stretched out, and impressed upon the hills were rectangular shapes, sharp and precise, each shape its own color An Iowa farmer looking out upon his handiwork must have sensed, it seemed to me, his enormous power and must have felt great pride. Here and there, along a river or on some steep slope, nature was allowed to hold forth—trees and grass and brush—but not to encroach. Then I drove onto the roads of the Fox community. Immediately nature leapt up: the terrain was formed of hills and bluffs and streams; trees were seen in any direction in small and large clusters and covering whole hills, and some reached high. In the spaces that remained, grass and weeds and brush threatened to reach as high. Growth was beneath me, around me on all sides, and overhead.

There, I recognized, was the difference. Passing through the countryside of white Iowa, one senses, as the Iowa farmer must sense, that he stands on top of what he sees, and a relationship is compellingly conveyed: man and his works. Entering the Fox community, one senses, as a Fox must sense, that he is enveloped.

I have described, as this third feature of the Fox kind of man, a set of ideas in his head about the nature of things—

Fox natural science, as it were. Fox ideas could, I supposed, be restated in terms of recurrent patterns of Fox behavior. Earlier I said the typical Fox was generous and circumspect. What third adjective would I add, thinking inductively (in imitation of Benedict) from the information at hand? It sounded strange to the English-speaking ear, but perhaps it should: *The typical Fox is harmonious.* In their behavior toward their natural environs, the Fox characteristically acted so as to sustain an enduring harmony.

These three adjectives—generous, circumspect, harmonious —seemed in combination illogical. That Fox strain for harmony, expressed in their relations with the natural environs, may in fact have been the very thing I saw when I described the Indians as circumspect, expressed then in their relations with one another. Indeed, even generosity may have been merely a third expression of the Fox strain for harmony. But illogical or not, I left the matter there.

In describing only these three features of the Fox kind of man, much of Fox life was, I thought, summed up. It began to be apparent to me why the boundaries which marked off "home" for the Fox were more abrupt than the boundaries most other men know. White Iowans leave the familiar places of their childhood with rarely more than occasional twinges of homesickness. But whenever a Fox went to Tama or beyond, he entered a new world of thought and behavior in which he must often have felt himself a stranger.

Similarly, a white man, entering the Fox community, entered a world of thought and behavior in many respects strange.

The neighbors of the Fox described Fox life as "unambitious" and "dependent"; those neighbors had, it seemed on close inspection, merely named one kind of man the Fox were not. I, having briefly tried to imitate Benedict, partially described the Fox life as "generous," "circumspect," "harmonious." That was a beginning, at least, of a description of the kind of man the Fox were—especially perhaps, that awkward-sounding last term, harmonious.

The neighbors of the Fox were estranged. So, then, was I. In the course of these brief and early inquiries, my estrangement began, ever so little it seemed, to give way.

4. The Big Impossible— Being a Man

I N THE late fall of 1952, events took over, not of my making but welcome. A group of Fox veterans of World War II became active and I, being a veteran, was drawn in. My Benedict-like inquiries continued for some while, but my new activities with the veterans, it turned out, were themselves a study, though logically different in kind. That logical difference, not the events themselves, soon pushed my earlier inquiries out of mind. A new mode of looking at the Fox took over.

This chapter is an anecdote about fifty young Fox Indians. It was very difficult for these fifty Fox veterans to find ways to act like men. This was not a matter of sex. This story is about another need males have, the world over: a need to find tasks that want doing, tasks that are seen by one's family and fellows as worthy and useful and appropriate for males, a need to express one's manhood by doing male work. How else might one feel the reward of being a worthy son or husband or father or elder? How else be a man? Such worthy male tasks were rare in this Indian community. Many Indian men seemed to sense this vacuum in their lives, and they strived, sometimes with desperation, to find ways to fill it. They were men, of course; they wanted to express the fact. For these reasons, the Fox veterans kept very busy throughout the fall, winter, and spring of 1952-53, building a veteran's club, and they kept me busy with them. They were trying to fill a void.

The women of the Fox seemed strong. They were usually busy; they appeared self-confident and capable when they went about the many household things that kept them busy. Their life was strenuous; usually there were several children, and the houses were crowded and often lacked running water to lighten the work. But they went about their tiring work and most seemed not unhappy.

In 1800 what were the Fox women doing? They were bearing children and caring for them; they were tending gardens of squash, beans, and corn; they were cooking; they were making clothes, utensils, household equipment. Much happened in the years since 1800. For example, all the material things the Fox came to use—tools and shelters and clothes and utensils—all these changed. But in 1952 Fox women still hoed gardens and cooked and sewed. The discontinuity in Fox life was great, but the women's work hardly showed it.

Women the world over have one large advantage over men in seeking purpose: they bear children. They have guaranteed to them this one function, than which nothing could be more important, for societies must produce new generations. By this single act a woman is able unmistakably to announce her womanliness and claim recognition of her female worth. In 1952 Fox women still bore Fox children.

Societies must invent analogous acts for men; they must reserve certain of their tasks for men, invest them with honor, and call them manly. Usually these tasks are important to social well-being; usually they are of some complexity and require learning and application. In doing them well, men announce their male worth.

In 1800 a Fox young man joined other young men for frequent hunts. They might trap for trade furs or stalk deer. In the summer they might ride out on the edge of the Great Plains to surround buffalo herds in the manner of Plains Indians. These tasks required knowledge learned from their fathers and required skill through application. The health of their families and community depended on them. It was honorable men's work.

In 1800 a Fox young man participated very little in the political deliberation of the village. But if a decision were made there for war, he, as a warrior, would perform a second honorable male task for his community and in doing it well he would serve his own reputation. As a young Fox entered his middle years, he joined more in political deliberation. If he had served well as a young hunter and warrior, he would already enjoy some honor. If also he displayed wisdom in deliberations, and if his deportment was increasingly more circumspect and unoffending, he could, during his advanced years, become a man of great influence.

During his middle years, too, a Fox man would learn the ritual knowledge of his kinsmen, as taught in ceremonial practice by the old men of the kin group. If he learned well, and if he was becoming a man to whom others listened in political deliberations, then he might as an old man come to enjoy the largest duty of all: as ritual head of his kin, he would hold in his mind the ritual knowledge deemed crucial to Fox survival and he would be, with the heads of other kin groups, one of the council of the tribe. In this most honored male work, he would come to be a kind of living symbol of the group who honored him.

Of all these, only one thing remained to a Fox young man in 1952: he could hope to become in his later years the ritual leader of his kin. But he could not hunt, and most of the economic things he could do were utterly detached from the community and were not therefore seen as especially manly or honorable. It was not irrelevant that a man was a good breadwinner, but a man's job had to mean more than that if it was to help him find himself as a man. He could not often fight; it was relevant when he did, as in World War II, but his efforts as a warrior were far removed, abstract, intangible. He could in his middle years enter tribal politics, but that was to dicker and wheedle with white men and be abused by Fox and was embarrassing more than honored. He could, then, look ahead twenty years to the time when he might become a ritual leader. Twenty years is a long time, and since the religious leaders no longer constituted a council and did not enjoy unusual secular influence, some of the reward in that was gone.

The attrition of the years on these male tasks had left a vacuum in Fox male life. It showed in 1952 in fifty young veterans, in their confustion and essential doubt about the meaning of their lives and about their place in their community.

During World War II these young men volunteered or were drafted. They were given farewell parties when they went to war. Almost all were in the infantry or parachute corps; some saw combat, more did not. Most saw much more of the world than they had before. They got to know white men in ways impossible before. Being an Indian was, if anything, a mark of some additional distinction. They were away from home and some were lonely; at least one would go off and "talk Indian—just to hear it." They were mustered out and came home.

There were welcome parties. To their families and friends they were literally returned warriors, and honored as such. There are Fox religious rituals that can be stopped only by a warrior who, at the right moment, strikes the drum and then recounts his war deeds; these veterans were asked to do that; the ritual was for them. So this manly role, warrior, could for a brief while be acted out, be lived in the presence of an audience who responded. The other Fox also told the veterans how much they were counting on them "to help," but were not able to say just how.

They came back, then, one by one, and lived for a few months in some glow of recognition and, perhaps, unreflecting confidence. But it was inevitable that the glow would pass. Having a social role means doing some social thing. There was nothing apparent for them to do as warriors, and so being a warrior soon became visibly empty. It was inevitable that they would attempt to fill that emptiness by finding social things for warriors to do.

Their move was to create an American Legion post; Number 703, it became, "The All-American Post." Previously several Fox young men had joined a post in nearby Tama. A federal law forbade the sale of liquor to Indians, and the Tama post, fearful of getting into trouble, asked the Indians not to drink. They left the Tama post and moved in 1948 to organize their own. They did so successfully; virtually all the young men joined, and they participated in parades, Memorial Day celebrations, and the like. By 1950, however, momentum dropped off, and for a year or so the Legion post did not do much.

In late summer, 1952, some of the men got the idea of converting an unused barnlike building into a meeting hall;

they wanted the hall to serve also as a social center for the community. Work began in the fall. Again most of the young men joined in. They elected officers and set about the rather expensive and complicated task of making a barn into a community hall. The people seemed pleased. This work-to-be-done got the post again on its feet; for almost a year it was a very lively affair.

At the beginning there was enough money in the post treasury to buy cement for a floor. One of the men brought down a tractor, others brought shovels and the like; the place was cleaned out, the dirt floor was leveled, and a cement company brought loads of mixed cement and dumped them. The men tamped and leveled. As they neared the end, a brush fire broke out on an adjoining hill, so they all ran out to help; the cement got very stiff. At the end, one part of the floor was a bit rough, but they had a good, dry floor and turned to other tasks, the treasury empty.

One way to make money in the Fox community was to have a "box social." Wives and mothers donated packed dinners of chicken, "fry-bread," and the like, and one of the young men (one who did not too much mind behaving in a banteringly aggressive way, which verged, in Fox eyes, on being unseemly) auctioned them off. The post provided coffee. People ate; then some of the older men gathered around a drum to sing while others, mostly the women, danced. By midnight, everyone had had fun and the post had enough money to buy gypsum board and to begin to finish the bare inside walls of the barn.

The young men fitted themselves into the work according to their various talents. As these men found themselves busy with the work at hand, many seemed to be transformed. Bill Walker was one. Earlier he had seemed colorless, but gradually that appearance of colorlessness was displaced. Meetings of the veterans, with Bill frequently acting as chairman, ran effectively to conclusions, by thoroughly Fox procedure. The men would gather, most within a half hour of the appointed time, stand about, gradually sit down in twos and threes chatting or joking. Some time later Bill would, in a voice almost inaudible, make a casual allusion to the subject matter that had made the meeting necessary; they were in the midst of refinishing the barn and were faced, say, with the decision of buying paint with the money left in the treasury or buying materials for a planned partition. The matter might be taken up; if not, then after some while an allusion would fall a second time from Bill's lips. Once the matter was taken up, Bill would say no more unless some question of fact were asked of him. Ultimately a group sentiment would be felt to have crystallized (the cue was when those who had had objections ceased to expres them), at which point Bill would say: "It's decided, then; we use the money for paint." And if there were minor loopholes in the judgment, he would mention them, systematically gathering up loose ends so as to make the decided course feasible.

Bill was, clearly, the embodiment of the "good Fox" in this particular realm—a man who knew well the requisites of leadership in a society where, in almost all contexts, any move to direct another, to boss, was considered an aggressive affront. But no one could have known about that talent—Bill himself could not have known it or long believed in it—except that the talent be expressed in work.

Similarly, another man was a good carpenter. Another, witty and known as a clown, took on the very ticklish job of sergeant-at-arms, "bouncer," he used to say, and carried it off without undue offense on the rare occasions it was required.

So it went; some months and several box socials later, the barn was finished, the walls painted, curtains up (courtesy of the women), linoleum on the floor, a pop cooler and propane stove installed, and a sign outside the door. Almost all the young men had invested time and money, some had invested a great deal. One could not say the work was pure, uncomplicated fun; it seemed probable, however, that the young men, looking back, felt good when they remembered those busy months.

Already, even as the construction was going on, the hall was a community center. At least once a week, on Sunday night, a dozen or so Fox families plus most of the Fox school-age boys and girls would come for Indian dancing. The men sang the Indian songs and drummed, and women danced. People bought pop and hamburgers and coffee, and the profits bought paint.

During these good months the young men were busy, doing work their friends and relatives thought good. During these few months they had found a way to be men.

The refinishing was complete in the spring, and the men decided to invite the legionnaires of the vicinity to hold one of their regional meetings in the new Fox Legion Hall—a formal opening of sorts. No doubt these Fox young men, through all the months of refinishing the barn, had often thought of that white audience of fellow veterans. But those had been busy months, with one event following hard upon another, and it was clear that the attention of the young men had been much more on their own community, who were right here through all of it, who now had a community center and therefore said good things about the veterans. Now that work was done, the Fox veterans thought again about those other veterans, their white neighbors, and so they invited them.

The invitation was a catalyst for one further bit of work. Finished? They looked again. They had overlooked the outside! There was the post hall: the inside gleamed, but the outside showed the weathered original white paint, badly chipped and peeling. So long as the minds of the young men had been turned toward each other and toward the community, no one had given this old paint a thought; the Indians do not usually attach great importance to tidiness, as mere appearance. But when the young men turned their minds to the white audience, they saw the building, for a moment, through white eyes. So they decided they ought to paint it. The planned opening was some weeks off, and no one seemed to have more than abstract enthusiasm for the work. Finally, one Sunday in July, when the arrival of the neighbor-veterans was but days away, my good friends stirred themselves and, in a flurry of work, painted the two sides that showed.

The formal opening came off well. Several of the neighboring legionnaires had taken personal interest in the post, helping now and again with procedural matters and the like. They were rightly impressed and the Fox young men rightly proud. But the formal opening of the hall was virtually the end of the post. From this point forward the young men were an organization without work to do; in other words, they were not an organization.

There were meetings, and in those meetings there was some casting about for something to do. Several times a young man, with an eye to the white models would suggest starting a drum and bugle corps; no one laughed, but no one bought any drums or bugles. Some were apparently willing, again following the outside models, to hunt for communists, but how one began was rather vague, so that too was dropped as quickly. The hall, as community center, continued to run well. There was no formal organization and none was necessary; people just came down and danced. The post sank back into inactivity and while nominally it continued to exist, practically it slowly died.

During these several months, through the fall, winter, and into the spring, I had been helping, I suppose, if one counts hammering nails and just generally being around; certainly I had been learning. Action anthropology sets out to help while learning and learn while helping, in equal emphasis. In these activities with the Fox veterans the two seemed in rather poor balance. Partly for this reason, I sought for reasonable activity in a few other directions. In the early spring, for example, we set in motion a small cooperative farming venture involving three Fox families on the few acres of farmland attached to the University's house, our residence; the venture was an experiment to test forms of interpersonal relations relatively strange to the Fox, and the results (some few months later) seemed to show that these forms of relationship held no evident promise for the community. Similarly, my wife and a score or so of teenage Fox girls grew cucumbers, which venture proved (weeks later) more about Iowa weather than about the Fox.

Through it all, however, my mind seemed largely pre-empted by those fifty veterans and their efforts, and what they seemed to mean. With the death of the All-American Legion Post #703, these men lost one of their few chances to be men— to proclaim and act out manliness through doing male work to an approving audience dear to them. So returned the emptiness.

A brief interlude such as those few months of good work could not bring large and permanent change to the young men, of course. Most had become inured to the emptiness of their male life. Most were able to grasp the brief relief and enjoy the fleeting sense of being, in that small way, men. One of them was not; long before, he had become more desperate than they; where others endured, he lashed out, at the white world, at Indians, and especially at himself. George Marlin (the name is fictitious, as all names have been, and the facts distorted) was a heavy drinker, often surly when drunk; many times he sobered up over coffee at our table, and each time, at some juncture, he would hold up his dark-skinned hand and say with hardly concealed aggressiveness: "That won't wash off." By a quirk of mischievous fate, many of the major forces that pulled at Fox society seemed to pull at him most directly: his father was a ritual head, a religious leader in the traditional religion, and George seemed to be his favorite apprentice; and his sister was married to a prominent local Christian. Similarly, George was intelligent and had learned technical skills under the G. I. Bill, but he was now working intermittently as a common laborer. Above all, he could not decide whether or not to be a Fox Indian.

As the months passed, one could watch George as he was dragged in his struggle for identity through mind-racking recurrent cycles which ran their course with slow inevitability in about three months. During an early phase of his cycle he would be withdrawn, almost invisible, utterly inactive. Slowly he would begin to stir, often by appearing at the Legion hall where, during those months of Legion activity, some of the young men could usually be found hammering or painting, and George would briefly lend a hand. Within a few days he would be completely caught up in Legion affairs, working all day every day, active in the planning, obviously enjoying himself. He had charm and wit during those few weeks. He talked often about "us Indians," what "we" do, and feel, and think, with the appearance of much pride. At these times he was very useful to the group. He relished certain tasks that most of the others found distasteful: for example, being the bantering, humorously aggressive master of ceremonies at the occasional fund-raising social events given by the veterans. He could better than anyone coax and needle people into playing or dancing or buying, to the Legion's profit.

George at these times was unusually energetic, but his energy, once he was working on some task, quickly began to break through the self-restraint every Fox needs, for self-control requires that one know who he is. As the days of activity moved along, he would with slow inevitability become impatient with his fellows, then irritable, then domineering. As this happened, the men began to withdraw from him. His aggression (for that is how the Fox viewed it) could not, according to their rules and practices, be met with counter-aggression: the Fox are circumspect. Such aggression was met by withdrawal from the offender, a tentative, informal ostracism; the men simply pretended not to see George or hear him. This reprimand from his fellows drove him, after some days, into the frantic third phase of his cycle. He became vocally "anti-Indian," abusive, often moved to a rooming house in nearby Tama, drank more than usual, fought when drunk, and spent most weekends in jail. After some weeks, physically exhausted and often swollen and bloody, George would return, withdrawn and inactive, to begin a new cycle. I was to see this painful cycle again, several weeks later.

The annual Pow-wow of August, 1953, caught George in an active, pro-Indian phase, but it was past its peak and he was sliding into his frantic, anti-Indian phase. The Pow-wow was the only occasion in the year when the community, almost to a man, explicitly announced and paraded its Foxness. There was, as far as there can be in this century, little ambivalence in the minds of most Indians during these few days each year. "We are Fox Indians," the women in effect asserted; perhaps the men said, rather, "We would like to be Fox Indians." All said together, we have these songs and these dances, and (sketchily) this history, and (implicitly) we are small and powerless and need your friendship. This year, as preparations were getting under way some four weeks in advance, George took no part. As the Pow-wow neared, he was asked to lend his technical skill in certain rather intricate building and repair, which he did, working hard for the last three days. During the Pow-wow itself, he was much in evidence, in the capacity of stage manager, conspicuously busying himself during the performances with the equipment, as if to underscore the fact that *he* was not out there dancing, yet not quite washing his hands of it. On the last night, he turned up at performance time, more than slightly drunk, dressed up in Indian Pow-wow dress but with so much paint and paraphernalia about his face as to render himself almost unrecognizable, and he danced and danced and danced, and the next day moved to the rooming house in Tama.

Nothing was clearer. The human animal cannot just be, but must be some social thing. The fact that one is born male only sets the problem. To be some social thing means to hold a set of social positions; but social positions are jobs to do, opportunities to act out, or they are nothing. Every man knows, from his own human experience, that the source of most human pleasures and human pain can be found in doing good, honored work, or in being frustrated in that human need. And frustration breeds anti-social, self-destructive mischief, which cannot fill the vacuum.

After the post was dead, those Fox young men seemed frequently to look back on the months during the fall, winter, and spring of 1952-53; from their conversation I thought they saw in those months of busy, good work a kind of model of what the whole Fox community might be again, in some better world. There was little of normal human buzz in the Fox community, and that was the pain of being an Indian.

I observed these unfolding events while participating in them over the better part of year. Through those months I was increasingly saddened, of course, as the unwashed truth about contemporary Indian life began to impress itself upon me, if only in outline. But my earlier sense of estrangement seemed to have gone away in large part, and I came to feel confident that in fact I might in some part do the impossible thing, might get an intellectual purchase on the complex confusion that is the life of this small human community and usefully describe it.

The two things—my reduced estrangement from Fox life and my increased sense of intellectual grasp of Fox life—were of course one and the same. These happy developments were, however, a windfall, the chance occurrence of a series of events of a special kind and my chance involvement in those events. By this windfall I had been propelled, mind and all, over some intellectual hurdle or hurdles, yet to be examined.

5. Notes in the Margin:
On Viewing Alien Ways

IT IS possible and necessary, now, to get down to funda-mentals, not about the Fox, but about those other men who had been hovering about, the white neighbors of the Fox, and that other observer of the Fox, the writer. One can, seventeen years later, step back and look at those ob-servers. Specifically, it is possible to get down to the question: what of a purely cognitive nature typically goes on inside the head of a Western man, when he looks at some tribal or peasant other, that typically estranges him? And it is possible, seventeen years later, to add the question: can one do anything about that?

To describe a human community is, on the face of it, impossible. Yet all men frequently do, of necessity, if only in familiar everyday surroundings; one could not live through an average day in his home community without, in some fashion, describing it to himself, thus to relate to it reasonably and effectively. There is some mystery as to precisely how this or that description comes about. This much is certain: no description can emerge except through prodigious mental activity (though that activity may be going on unknown). All such description is a summing up of some kind, and all summing up involves the illusion that one sees recurrent happenings. But among the unfolding complex sets of raw observable happenings "out there," there is no self-evident recurrence, only a sequence of ultimately unique events.

Probably uniqueness itself cannot be seen by a human mind. Similarity can be seen, but to a single mind at one time, only a few kinds of similarity. Thus, of the observable goings-on in a community only the smallest fraction can get recorded by the mind, and every description is an artifact composed of a few happenings, which seem to the observer similar in one or another respect to a few other happenings. There is of course a near infinity of options as to what features will determine these similarities and great arbitrariness in their choice. One is accustomed to calling these mental gymnastics "describing" and to calling the resulting artifacts of mind "descriptions;" these pages will perpetuate that comfortable myth.

A crucial, saving feature about human action—a quality of human behavior that allows description at least a good start— is this: the actors themselves imagine one event to be like another. It may not really happen twice that a given male, forty years old, brief case in one hand, leans over, puts his other hand on the head of a seated female seven years old, and touches his closed lips to her cheek, this at 5:30 P.M. January 5, 1970, in the front room of a house they both occupy, etc., etc. But to the members of that society in which that man resides it does seem unmistakably and frequently to occur that "fathers kiss daughters." Each of these three words stands for a publicly recognized class of things: many unique individuals are seen to be fathers, many unique actions are seen to be kissing, and many other unique individuals are seen to be daughters of fathers. Thus to the men of that society such arrays of individuals and actions seem alike, and therefore, to many social purposes, are alike.

Description requires prodigious selection. Of the observable goings-on in a community, some fraction gets through when a Western man confronts the goings-on in his familiar Western surroundings. Probably some other fraction gets through when he looks at some culturally alien people. In the former case, the observer will already know, often without even knowing that he knows, that the words "fathers" and "kiss" and "daughters" stand for three publicly recognized classes of things. In the latter case, the observer cannot at the outset know whether that culturally different people hold in their minds these three classes of things, and he may, not quite knowing that he does not know, describe after a fashion by unconsciously circumventing the missing facts: "This people," he might say, "are affectionate." An observation of just this logical kind is the likely report to fall from the lips or pen of most Western men when they look at some alien life. (The Fox are unambitious, dependent, generous, circumspect, harmonious.) That is, the information that gets through in the two cases, in familiar surroundings and in alien places, will be different not only in amount but almost certainly will be different in kind.

Nondescriptions

Some descriptions by Western men of non-Western others are merely self delusions—nondescriptions—and these can quickly be dispatched. The neighbors of the Fox when they described the Indians described negatively: they said the Fox were *not ambitious*. When white Iowans reported that the Fox were not ambitious, they informed us that the Indians did not exhibit (for example) that particular array of practice toward the land which a white Iowan would recognize as ambition. And that, as earlier noted, merely named one kind of man the Fox was not. Nondescriptions emerge from this logical trap: one has, say, a number of items, a basket of rubber balls; if it is known that some balls are red and all others are blue it makes no difference whether one reports of a certain ball that it is blue or that it is not red. But if the colors of the balls cover the total spectrum, one says little by naming any one color one ball is not. The Fox, white Iowans said, was not some one kind of a man—so out of the many kinds he could be, those observers named one kind he was not. One could also safely assert that the Fox is not a Japanese kind of man who must create in his landscape disciplined beauty.

"Ambition" is an item from some unexamined list of behavior familiar to one group of Western man; it covers very diverse actions and is seen as a single category of behavior because the cultural tradition of that group has so defined it. To most Westerners the word unites actions that to the Fox must have semed to fall into several quite distinct Fox categories: working energetically (which in certain contexts the Fox appeared to do), seeking higher economic status (which the Fox probably saw as puzzling or as indecent depending on who, relatively, was losing status), subjecting nature (which most Fox would probably have found almost incomprehensible,) and so on. Bound by that Western term, the mind asked whether the usual Fox was ambitious or not. And the answer had to be No. Thus was named one kind of man he was not. Later that other observer of the Fox, the writer, asked: what *was* a Fox, and one answer was: a Fox was harmonious. That sounded strange to Western ears; it should.

Out of some unnamed array of all the kinds of men who might exist, the neighbors of the Fox named one kind of man he was not. At best, then, the Fox were left undescribed, still inscrutable. But worse and most likely, they were made by that negative term inconceivable. The description of the Fox as "not ambitious" allows one logically to suppose they may have had motivations in some other direction, perhaps like the motivations of a religious hermit. The implication is, however, very strong to Western ears that they were men devoid of motivation altogether. Taking that conclusion literally, one could perhaps imagine in the abstract that some individual Fox might have been reduced by extreme mental disorder to a wholly inert state; but such a man would have been quite beyond one's ability to imagine, and in that sense, nonhuman. The truth value of a description which renders a people inscrutable or inconceivable is, of course, zero. In contrast, the assertion that the Fox were harmonious permits one grossly to recognize that the Fox intent was to preserve some sort of harmony with the land and the universe of things. One can perhaps imagine himself entertaining such a view and behaving accordingly.

The trouble is, of course, that such nondescriptions are so very easy, undemanding of the observer. But the way toward truth is much assisted by a simple rule of thumb: one never describes an alien people by naming what they are not. That is, whenever in a description of an alien other the words "are not" or "lack" or prefixes and suffixes like "un-" or "-less" come into the mind or fall from the pen, warning bells should ring, for the chances are strong that, at that juncture, the people have been left undescribed and perhaps rendered inconceivable.

This rule should apply whether one finds himself describing by naming the material things a people don't possess, or the customs they don't practice, or the beliefs they don't entertain, or the offices they don't have. This simple rule, if applied, would eliminate out of hand a remarkable proportion of everyday talk and writing about the world's tribal peoples and peasants, and it would make life a bit easier for the Fox and for the neighbors of the Fox as well.

The Descriptive Notion: Character

Another white man, this writer, looked at the Indians and came to descriptive thoughts about them: the Fox were generous, circumspect, harmonious. It is possible to turn now, seventeen years later, to think about those thoughts, not about their content but about the underlying logical form, the habits of mind, that shaped that thinking.

One needs a verbal label, so let us call this mode of description formed by the notion of "character." The imagery which suggests this label is the common usage that when any man, for whatever unexamined reasons—habit, moral persuasion, neurotic compulsion—*acts* consistently in describable ways, he is said to have that particular character. The notion of character, like all such forms, selectively screens observation in a special fashion and arranges selected items of information in a special fashion. We must now attempt to discover and make explicit those two underlying habits of mind: what kinds of phenomena were selectively observed? and by what devices were those selective observations sorted and ordered? The net result is that a human community comes to be described as a kind of man.

"The Fox," said that observer, "is generous," which is to

say that Fox men in some frequency large enough to impress the observer seemed to give things to other Fox men.

Fox life, simply because it was one form of human life, must necessarily have been many visible things. Infants were born, and the community experienced attendant fear and joy; infants grew and learned; young people courted and married; old people grew feeble; men died; the human life career, in whatever special forms the Fox knew it, recurrently unfolded. Each year, too, some regular series of events unfolded with the Iowa seasons: the spring planting of the many gardens and the few farms, and the fall harvest; a round of religious events and recreational "Indian games"; occasional councils of importance; an annual Pow-wow each August; at least all these. Of all that, some got through, fixed itself on the mind of the observer, and that which got through was so arranged that the summary sentence emerged: "The Fox is generous." How?

What got through was an embarrassingly simple matter: acts of giving and other acts of not giving. It is as if Fox acts of giving had occurred frequently enough to impress themselves on the observer, and that he then put on a pair of glasses which "saw" in all events acts of giving or acts of not giving, that he then scanned the Fox scene for some while and concluded that the frequency of giving was noteworthy (though without counting).

On the other hand, some Fox behavior did not get through. Who gave, and to whom, in terms of individual Fox men? For all the observer knew (at least, for all he could have demonstrated) all the giving was the doing of a small handful of Fox lunatics who were forever handing things out. Or, who gave to whom in terms of social position? For all the observer could have demonstrated, most of that giving was the doing of a handful of the very poor who gave conspicuously with some ulterior motive, or of a handful of the white-oriented Fox who had been told bible stories and had taken them at face value. Or, finally, and more literally to the point, Fox reactions to giving did not get through: the obvious or more subtle indications of approval, disapproval, surprise, indifference, whatever, on the part of those who received and, more importantly perhaps, on the part of other Fox who stood by. For all the observer could have demonstrated, these Fox reactions were unknown.

That observer, through common sense and out of common human experience, might in fact have known in a rough way much of this screened-out fact. The point, however, is that the descriptive notion of character did not force him to know, did not forcibly protect him from error.

The descriptive notion of character, then, is seen to have selected out, in this instance, acts of giving and acts of not giving. All such descriptive notions also arrange in some manner various items of selected information. With the notion of character, such an arranging is already accomplished, in that there is but one choice: one makes, as it were, a pile of giving behavior, another pile of nongiving behavior, and if the first seems high enough, concludes, "The Fox is generous."

Description by the notion of character is, thus, opaque, not very illuminating. One does not quite know what, in fact, Fox men—different Fox men in different Fox situations—do. Still less does one know whether these things are done out of habit, moral persuasion, neurotic compulsion, all these, none of them, or whatever.

Yet that white observer, the writer, was curiously drawn to this manner of describing. "The Fox are generous, circumspect, harmonious." Why the attraction? First, in such a context, one must do something; second, describing by this mode is easy; third, the results provide an illusory comfort.

Surprises are assaults to a human mind. The life of an alien people is to an observer necessarily full of surprise, and such nearly total assault is quite beyond human tolerance. A few men can, perhaps, simply close themselves off. But most minds must act otherwise; their desperately felt need is to reduce the incidence of surprise. In varying degrees Peace Corpsmen, missionaries, drifters, tourists, and anthropologists all suffer the same assault and must similarly seek relief from it. All set out to describe people, to sum up life, and thus to reduce the incidence of surprise— if for no other reason than that today be psychologically more comfortable than yesterday.

Under such assault, Western minds, it seems, often grasp unaware the device here called the notion of character. It is facile: the notion acts drastically and with undemanding simplicity to select a few kinds of fact from all that impinges, provides a manner of sorting and summarizing these facts, and thereby brings about a measure of intellectual order.

This measure of order carries immediate comfort by reducing the sense of surprise: "Ah ha! You see. He gave that to him." Similarly, "The Fox is circumspect." This descriptive sentence is ever more comforting, since in Fox life the pile of circumspect behavior is high to the virtual exclusion of behavior not circumspect: "In all those months I have never heard a Fox shout in anger." This last, however, is a result of the accidental fact that Fox life happens to be unusually monolithic in one respect. The comfort is simply there in greater or lesser degree, unexaminable. The notion of character, as here defined, can go no further.

Nondescription by the Notion of Character

Confronted with the confusion which is an alien life, the mind must do something. Description by the notion of character is easy and comforting. Nondescription, which proceeds by naming things a people do not have, customs they do not practice, beliefs they do not entertain, is also easy. The two together, nondescription by the notion of character, is undemanding of the observer and a guaranteed source of total comfort to him.

The neighbors of the Fox said: "The Fox are unambitious and dependent." It is evident: not only were these nondescriptions, they were nondescriptions formed by the notion of character. The Fox, displayed some very large piles of "not-ambitious" and "not-independent" behaviors.

These observers came to the Fox, two pairs of glasses already in hand. By the mere fact that ambitious behavior and independent behavior are complex categories more or less precisely defined in the unfolding of the Western cultural tradition, it was virtually guaranteed that no Fox on any series of Fox occasions would have behaved in ways that fully fit either of them. Those observers were guaranteed huge piles of unambitious behavior and dependent behavior and a virtual absence of their opposites.

Description formed by the notion of character alone may be empirically confirmed some of the time or much of the time, either of which in different ways being a comfort. Nondescription by the notion of character is certain to be empirically unassailable and powerfully comforting.

But more: the observer is doubly comforted. Description by the notion of character loads the dice in favor of things bizarre and morally noisy; the full welter of behavior in a human community competes for the observer's attention. Initial impressions must break through in the first place, to cause the observer to look for one sort of behavior rather than another. Behavior that by the observer's own experience as shaped by his cultural tradition seems bizarre or morally noisy would, on the face of it, compete well for his attention. Nondescriptions present no hindrance to this bias. So the observer ends, often, by naming the virtues, the morally correct behaviors, that are *not* in evidence. "The Fox are unambitious, dependent." This is doubly comforting since it serves the observer also as self-congratulation.

Nondescriptions by the notion of character are undemanding of the observer, indeed seem "natural." They typically go unchallenged empirically and thus totally remove surprise; in that sense they comfort. They may frequently focus only on virtues and thereby serve for self-congratulation, thus doubly comfort. *Nondescription by the notion of character is a lure and a delusion and, once one has slipped into that procedure, a steel trap.* The neighbors of the Fox did not play games with the words *unambitious, dependent.* It seems rather that these words—and the nondescriptions by the notion of character that lay behind these words—played games with the neighbors of the Fox.

The trouble is, of course, that nondescription by the notion of character seems certain to estrange. Description by the notion of character is at best opaque. Nondescription leaves a people inscrutable. The two together so dimly reflect what a community is about as virtually to remove the observer from his humane common sense. He cannot relate because he cannot see enough to relate to. Thus we got the destructive circle relating the Fox and their neighbors of actions and reactions shaped in substantial part by words; at least, without those words, the circle would not be. The circle is estrangement, Tama style.

What of a purely cognitive nature typically goes on inside the heads of Western men when they look at some tribal or peasant other that estranges them from him? The answer, of course, is: the notion of character, and especially those damnable nondescriptions by the notion of character. These estrange. And can one do anything about it? The remarkable fact is that devices of mind that promise to lead to adequate description of alien life are altogether commonplace among Western men. Many manners of describing are effectively and habitually deployed every day, without conscious self-direction but with great agility, by every normal man in the course of his usual goings and comings inside his home community.

A man wishes, say, to propose some action to the governing body of his political club. He has long since "filed" in mind that the club has a set of constituted offices and procedures; thus he is able, as he acts, to think of the club as a system of positions and incumbents and rules for appropriate conduct in those positions, and to act accordingly. He has also long since noted that the club chairman seems compulsively energetic, that another member seems unusually timid, so he acts with those facts of personality or temperament in mind. These and several other kinds of understanding of the world around him are held in mind, put there by mental devices that, typically unbidden, select and order for him the impinging phenomena: the club is seen as if it were a system of personnel, seen again as if it were an array of personalities, and so on. He brings into play such a series of devices first one and then another, unreflectively as he moves through any day, in a manner that, if only we understood it better, would surely resemble a very good juggling act. All those devices, each doing the work it can do, help put that wealth of detail into an order, or a complex series of orders, adequate to hold them in mind.

However, these commonplace devices of mind do not frequently get deployed when the same Western man chances to look across a cultural boundary. Minds seem curiously to freeze on one such device—"these people are unambitious and dependent and generous and circumspect"—like a car unable to get out of a rut. Thus it seems necessary to bring forward the other commonplace devices, to name them, and thus to help permit deploying them self-consciously in alien contexts. The main need, that is, in a world that closes in and thus demands accurate perception is not intellectual invention by scholars. (That there is anything unusually intellectual or inventive in the basic "methods" of the social sciences is, in any event, mere conceit.) Rather, the need appears to be an increase of introspective awareness about the commonplace workings of the usual agile mind.

One such alternative device has already entered these pages, in gross outline, running through the anecdote about the Fox veterans. There, words like social position, role, and organization, occurred; these words selected and ordered that particular ebb and flow of Fox behavior. I shall, as others do, call this device of mind description by the notion of social structure, and to more description by this device I now turn. The device itself, and others, will be examined later in these pages.

6. Fox Social Structure

I N JULY 1953 my wife and I were joined by other fellow students from Chicago. They went about their various tasks; I was probably somewhat withdrawn from them, preoccupied.

I had learned from working with the veterans that Fox young men found it difficult to find ways to be men, to demonstrate to themselves and their fellows worthiness in doing male work. They found it difficult, that is, to be sons and fathers and husbands, to fill these and other male positions in ways that were recognized as worthy.

But all these social positions existed in the Fox community, and Fox men were "in" them. My question became: why was filling the positions not rewarding? To answer, it was necessary first to learn something of the total array of Fox social positions and then to determine the systematic way those positions related one to the other—to describe, that is, the social structure of Fox society. This meant that I had to learn to think of the Fox community as a complex system of social positions into and out of which men moved as occurred the events that made up a Fox day or year or lifetime.

Pushing out of mind everything else I knew or thought I knew, I had to view the Fox community as an elaborate system for continually sorting and resorting the Fox as personnel. What enduring structure was visible there? What system of social positions organized Fox affairs and how were Fox individuals brought into the positions that others left, so that the system endured? A close analogue would be to describe a factory by naming the jobs and positions in it, the chain of command among these social slots, and by noting how the factory recruits and retires its manpower. Sol Tax asked these questions when he was among the Fox in the 1930s; Walter Miller continued this work. I found myself reading and bringing this earlier work of others to bear on what I saw of Fox life.

Sol Tax had written of the formal system of Fox social structure, and those facts of Fox life came compellingly into focus for me in mid-summer of 1953 when I was invited to attend an annual religious rite, a ceremony of one of the Fox clans.* Each year during the summer months there was a round of ceremonial feasts in which each of the several Fox clans took its turn being the host to the remaining clans; the host clan sang while the others danced, and the host prepared a feast for the others to enjoy. This was the traditional Fox religion. There had been a Christian mission in the community for two generations and perhaps half the families

* An earlier description of this ritual is included in my chapter, "Social Structure," in James Clifton, ed., *Introduction to Cultural Anthropology* (Houghton, Mifflin Co., Boston, 1968).

went to one or another of the various mission activities, but only two or three families attended the mission exclusively, rejecting the clan ceremonies.

Each Fox clan owned one or more sacred packs, bundles of sacred items. These sacred items represented salient events in Fox history, remote and not so remote; for example, the skin of an animal or bird, a Union Jack, a weapon. The packs were protected through the years and handled with respect. During a clan's ceremonial feast its pack was undone and laid out as a kind of altar before which the people sang and danced. Each pack, in turn, "owned" a certain ritual. The older members of a clan knew the large set of songs, which required most of a day to be sung, and knew their proper sequence.

That summer day in 1953 was the appointed time for the ritual of a pack. The clan that owned the pack began in the morning to bring quantities of meat obtained at Tama stores, and varicolored Indian corn grown in Fox gardens; men tended the cooking in large cast iron pots over open fires. Most of the community gathered, men, women, and children sat and stood under the trees or sat in cars. Everyone was relaxed, chatty but not boisterous; children were scolded if their play became too loud. By mid-morning, men from the host clan began singing inside the clan house, a rectangular plank house with an earth floor. One of the singers had a small tight drum and others had notched sticks upon which they made sounds in rhythm as with rasps; they sat in a group, cross-legged, at one corner of the clan house on a waist-high bench that ran full length along each side. Small groups of other Fox of all ages drifted in, listened a while, then left to return later. With some of the songs there was restrained dancing—a line of men and women who moved in a circle or danced in place. Between songs, singers joked a bit at the expense of one whose voice had cracked, or had threatened to give out; there was some stretching of cramped legs. The songs went on for an hour or two; then the community was served the stew of meat and corn, in wooden bowls. Members of the host clan had not eaten since the day before and still did not eat. Then more songs and more dancing. Finally, in late afternoon, the ritual ended. The community moved off. The host clan then sat down together and broke its fast. Then the clansmen disbanded to their homes.

I said the clan "owned" the sacred pack; more accurately, they carried the burden of that pack and its ceremony for the community. In this ceremony the people did not ask specific help of the supernatural beyond very general wishes for life itself, nor did they confess moral wrongs. The songs seemed, rather, to assert simply that this or that supernatural force existed. In performing its appointed ritual, the clan acquitted some Fox obligation to the order of things and reaffirmed for the Fox their place and their duties in that larger cosmic order.

Since the Fox had organized themselves for such an activity they must have utilized some system of ties that connected the men to their fellows. Sol Tax had much earlier shown that the Fox frequently used kinship ties. As I observed this clan ceremony, the Fox use of Fox kinship became tangibly evident. Every Fox was tied to every other Fox through blood or marriage, and this clan ceremony was organized by the resulting web of kinship. Kin ties carried obligations. Like most Americans, I saw fairly clearly the set of obligations entailed in being an American father to one's sons; my obligations seemed less clear and less imperative as an American uncle or nephew. With the Fox, Tax had shown, most kin ties carried with them obligations that, relative to American experience, were more clear and more imperative. It was in terms of these kin obligations that the Fox cooperated or did not, exerted influence or deferred to others, gave or received, joked or became soberly respectful, all this in the unfolding of the ceremonial clan feast.

Sol Tax had shown that to calculate how one man was related to another, the Fox made discriminations different from those we know. For example, most Fox had several relatives they called by a single term that was translated as "father": his father and all the brothers of that man. That seemed strange, but it should occur to us that there is no self-evident, compelling reason for white Americans to name as identical two distinct individuals, for example, one's mother's sister and father's sister, both of whom we call "aunt." The Fox called several men "father"; we call several women "aunt."

Human kinship systems are sets of such classifications of individuals variously connected to each other by genealogy and marriage. It is evident that there is some arbitrariness in how a society opts to arrange these clumpings and separations. When a man calls two individuals by the same kinship term, he generally senses a set of similar obligations toward them and enjoys a set of similar rights or privileges, and when he calls two individuals by different terms he senses contrasting rights and obligations toward them. If my child can ask one aunt for a nickel he can generally ask any equally accessible aunt for a nickel, and he is expected to say "thank you" with much the same intonation and demeanor to each of them.

The complex array of our familiar classification of kinsmen can be briefly shown in diagram. Figure I shows some of the relatives of a hypothetical American male called Ego. This American way of reckoning is called "bilateral," meaning that a man has the same kinds of kin connections with his mother's relatives as with his father's.

Figure I also shows some of the kin connections of a hypo-

Figure I.

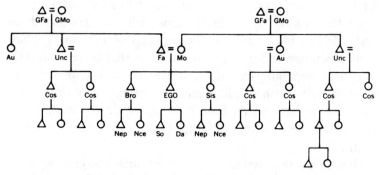

Selected American kinship terms.

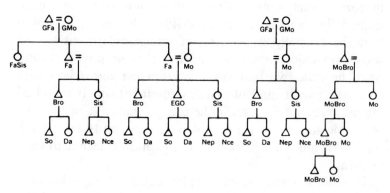

Selected Fox kinship terms in translation (after Tax 1955).

Figure II.

Two patrilineal lines of Fox kin.

EGO'S patrilineal kin:

The patrilineal kin group of EGO'S mother:

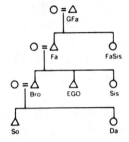

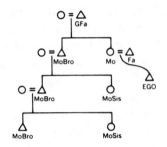

Key to Abbreviations

Father	Fa	Uncle	Unc	Niece	Nce
Mother	Mo	Brother	Bro	Son	So
Grandfather	GFa	Sister	Sis	Daughter	Da
Grandmother	GMo	Cousin	Cos	Mother's sister	MoSis
Aunt	Au	Nephew	Nep	Mother's brother	MoBro

Symbols

△: Male
○: Female
=: Marriage relationship

Note: Many relatives are omitted on both charts; those included are the minimum number that reveal the kinship pattern. Relatives not named on the American kinship diagram are "outside" the system in the sense that, in the usual mobile situation of most American families, they are rarely encountered and require no standard terms.

thetical Fox male, but named according to Fox reckoning. Some relatives that we lump together (our father's sister and our mother's sister, our "aunts") the Fox thought of as two different kinds of relative and called by two different terms; and some relatives that we distinguish (our father and his brothers, our "uncles") they considered as basically the same kind of relative and called by a single term, "father."

All these terms were the terms of everyday Fox use. Most Fox could carry in their minds the American reckoning and can say to a white man, "she is my cousin." But usually that was an on-the-spot calculation, so as not to confuse the white man.

Of course, a Fox, when he called two or more men by a single term, which we translate as "father," did not thereby confuse his biological father and that man's brother any more than Americans confuse their father's sister and mother's sister when they call both aunt; the single Fox term denoted a common set of obligations.*

This Fox system of reckoning kin had its own internal logic. The clans, I said, carried responsibilities for the ceremonial observations of the Fox religion. At birth every Fox was automatically assigned to a clan; for virtually every Fox it was the clan of his father (though later, individuals might be ceremonially adopted into a second or third clan). A clan, then, was basically made up of a few old men, their sons and daughters, their sons' children (but not their daugh-

* Translating Fox terms into English is misleading; obviously the Fox term *uswa* translated here as "father," could not have to a Fox the same range of meaning as the English word has to an English-speaking person. The usage in establishing these translations is simply this: one encounters the Fox term *uswa* first as Eco applies it to his biological father; one translates it as "father"; then when the same term is encountered the second or third time the early translation is kept. The term, to a Fox, might roughly translate as "males of my line one generation older than I am." The remaining translations should be thought of in the same way.

ters' children), and so on, the descendants of those few old men down through the male line—clan membership was "patrilineal." Since every Fox, man or woman, went at birth into a clan, the total Fox population formed a series of clans.

Figure II is a rearrangement of data in Figure I, showing the kin of an average Fox man. No new facts are added, but by this rearrangement the logic of the system is revealed. This new arrangement shows two lines of Ego's patrilineal kin. Ego is first shown among his own (his father's) line of relatives; within this line he had several kinds of kin, distinguished by sex and generation. These were Ego's fellow clansmen, and with these relatives, in terms of his various obligations to them and theirs to him, he cooperated in such things as the performance of the clan's ceremonial burden. But Ego also looked out upon a second line of kinsmen, the patrilineal line of kin to which his mother belonged, also shown in Figure II; she was a member (determined at her birth) of the clan of her father. These relatives of Ego were to him less central; for example, during a ceremony performed by his own clan, his mother and these her clansmen were no more than guests. There was accordingly less necessity for Ego to distinguish among them, and some necessity to lump them together; thus most of them were grouped as two kinds of kin according to their sex—the males were called "mother's brother" and the females were called "mother's sister," irrespective of their age and generation.

In short, Tax had shown that these kin terms reflected a sorting that went on recurrently in Fox society. For certain purposes, the total population arranged itself into a set of clans. Each clan was in turn composed of a few lines of patrilineal kin. The way any one person—the hypothetical Ego in our charts—referred to his relatives reflected the way he saw them sorted into these patrilineal lines: his own line (the line of his father), and his mother's patrilineal line. We

could look wider afield and diagram the patrilineal line of
EGO's father's mother and that of his mother's mother; most
of the relatives in both these lines were called by EGO grandfather and grandmother, again irrespective of age. (The Fox
recognized some humor in the fact that most adults had
"grandfathers" who are infants.)

In this manner the Fox elected to arrange themselves to
accomplish certain tasks, one of which was the round of clan
ceremonial feasts. A clan feast was not an elaborate event
in its physical arrangements: A day had to be set; food had
to be collected; on the morning of the ceremony a fire had to
be arranged and the cooking begun; the guest clans had to
be fed; finally, the host clan had to eat. All this required
some coordination of effort, but relatively simple *ad hoc*
arrangements probably could have gotten these tasks accomplished. As I watched the unfolding of the clan ceremony
that summer day, I came to recognize a further requisite for
clan feasts that was not so simply come by: ritual knowledge.
The ceremony proper consisted of a series of songs which
together lasted no less than four hours. Most of these were
sung only on the occasion of the feast itself, that is, once a
year; and there was no rehearsal. Each song, and the proper
sequence of all the songs, had to be known. During the
ceremony there were appropriate occasions for prayers. At
certain times people were to dance, at other times not. And
all this had ritual meanings that were not to every Fox
self-evident.

The lineal arrangement of Fox kinship provided a measure
of assurance that this ritual knowledge would be acquired
in each generation. The patrilineal clans were deathless; men
were born into them and men died out of them, but the
groups endured. It was the clans that owned the sacred
packs. The question of ownership was thereby securely ar-

ranged, for all time, insofar as this is possible in the human world. The owning of a pack was, of course, but a material reflection of the fact that in the clan rested the ritual knowledge necessary for the performance of the ceremony of that pack. Upon one old man, the clan head, rested the ultimate responsibility for holding that knowledge in his mind. Many other older men of the clan would also have committed the knowledge to memory, and each of these had sons and grandsons to whom the knowledge would be passed. These young boys, always the same group except for births and deaths, heard and heard again the performance of this ritual, once each year as they matured, and they joined in the performance each year when they became men. There was in this arrangement some assurance that when a clan head died others would be prepared to take his place.

I thus came grossly to see the Fox community as an arrangement of personnel, a system for assigning all individuals to an array of social places to perform some of the community's work. In 1953 the clan ceremonies were the only purpose for which the Fox formally arranged themselves as lineal kin groups, but earlier, it appeared, this arrangement was employed in other contexts, especially for purposes of arriving at political decisions—to fight or not, to move the village or not.

For these political purposes, the males had the major responsibility; the headmen of the several clans formed a council; one clan head was the tribe's civil or peace chief, another was the war chief, and there were a few other offices. Ranging down from each of these headmen were the male members of their respective clans. In this arrangement for political work, I found concretely illustrated that further point about the nature of a community seen as an enduring structure: kinship was more than the sorting of men into groupings; in the Fox community, as in tribal societies generally, each kinship relation was typically a set of clear and specific obligations and rights.

Within Ego's lineal kin group, as we saw, each man was to Ego brother or father or grandfather or son or grandson. These represented altogether three pairs of relationships: grandfather to grandson, father to son, brother to brother. Rights and duties were entailed in each paired relationship. Brothers were expected to be comradely but to show some restraint (for instance, it was unseemly for brothers to talk in each other's presence about sex or to joke boisterously). A Fox son was expected to respect and obey his father, and a father had the right to require his son to fast when he disobeyed or otherwise behaved improperly; theirs was a mildly disciplinary relationship. On the other hand, when a father exercised discipline against his son, the grandfather was expected to take the side of his grandson, to mitigate the punishment and to give advice more mildly; his was a more kindly and supportive role.

There appeared thus to be within this body of men a nice balance between discipline and unity, both of which were necessary if the group was to act effectively. Clearly, influence and authority flowed consistently in this set of relations from old to young, but not through the exercise of constraint alone. The young men knuckled under, but usually without a strong sense that their sentiments were ignored or willfully violated, for there was always sure recourse to grandfather when parental authority was unwise or abusive.

Thus these three kinds of relations within each lineal group—brother to brother, father to son, grandfather to grandson—once formed a basic channel for the flow of influence and authority when the total Fox population set itself to the task of making a political judgment. The Fox required that most of their political decisions be unanimous. The operation of such a web of relations within each lineal group helped to bring the sentiments of younger men into line with the sentiments of the older within each lineal group. This virtually guranteed an effective unanimity within each lineal group, and that made the task of arriving at unanimity in the total Fox community somewhat less overwhelming than it might otherwise have been.

By 1953 this structure for political action was no longer in use. A generation before, the traditional council having become inoperative, the Fox adopted a new organization involving an elected council of seven. The deliberations within the new tribal council were still very much as the older deliberations must have been: speeches were soft, direct argument was rare, decisions were almost invariably made by unanimous vote. All this had come to be couched in terms of *Robert's Rules of Order*, but it made no essential difference. However, this elected council did not systematically articulate with the community. Each council man had kin, but his webs of kin did not reach all the community in an orderly or usable manner. No equivalent system of non-kin relations, thus no new web of influence and authority, had yet emerged to replace the old. It followed that community wide unanimity had become rare, which is to say that effective political decisions were no longer made.

These observations of Fox organization for ritual and politics, past and present, showed me, as it had earlier shown others, that the Fox system of kinship reckoning had its own logic. Indeed, wherever patrilineal descent groups are used to get work done, the basic configuration of kinship is found—not always, but remarkably often. The archetype of this configuration is called by anthropologists the "Omaha" system, having been first encountered among that tribe of Indians.

I have shown only a few of the kin connections the Fox employ, and a full description of the enduring structure which was the Fox community would include much more. I had seen aspects of Fox organization for part of their religious life. Other parts of Fox religious ceremonial were organized by voluntary association, for example, in the Medicine Society. In Fox economic life labor had to be divided and goods had to be distributed and consumed; again certain social positions and groupings, mainly determined by kinship, were used for these purposes, and again there were notions about proper conduct, economic rights, and obligations entailed in those positions. Similarly, there were Fox structures available for education in the broadest sense—the socialization and training of the next generation—or for leisure, and for other such categories of group life.

One Fox organizational device systematically cross-cut family and kinship, age and sex, and all other groupings. By the simple expedient of assigning each child in every family alternatively to first one and then a second category (called *tokan* and *kishko*—the words have no other clear meaning), the total Fox population or any segment of it stood ready to form two camps, as the occasion arose that made this division appropriate or useful. Competitive games were such an occasion; personal competition, even at play, was a delicate matter to the Fox, and these two categories provided two sides automatically and impersonally. Even very young boys who might spontaneously break into a race often fell back on these ready made categories, as the first to reach the mark called out, "The *tokans* won." Probably this division was earlier used in war, obviously a highly competitive activity.

Indeed, Fox social structure even told the Fox with whom they should joke. Public behavior between Fox men and women was typically very restrained, yet Fox men could frequently be seen engaging in unrestrained joking with women, married and unmarried; the jokes always had flirtatious, quite open sexual references. It was not difficult to discover that these men were joking only with certain women, namely the sisters of their wives. Also, one learned easily that it was obligatory for a man to joke thus when he met his sister-in-law. Traditionally, Fox marriages were arrangements between two families that created bonds and obligations between those two families. But if a man's wife died, the forms of cooperation that had become habitual and useful between the two families were disrupted. So the Fox had another rule: if one's wife died, it was preferred that one take her sister as a second wife, in order to preserve the ties between the two families. It followed: the sister of one's wife was, potentially, one's future wife, which created potential stress: untimely romantic inclination toward the sister-in-law, jealousy on the part of the wife. The situation came to be handled by trial and error over the generations. Joking in human affairs is often a form of avoidance. It is difficult to maintain intense sentiments when one is caused to play the buffoon, so when a Fox man encountered his sister-in-law he joked about his passion.

Taking all this together, I was able to envisage a series of schematic pictures: One Fox mode of sorting overlay the next, the whole community shifting from one articulation to a second to a third as occasions came and went, the totality an elaborate system for continually sorting and resorting the Fox population. By this social structure the Fox organized themselves for the work, play, and worship that was still Fox life. Individuals died out, others were born and were caused to assume appropriate positions on appropriate occasions. The social structure endured.

So Fox social structure endured, in large part. Sundry social positions existed and could by Fox be named. People were "in" the various positions. The Fox young veterans were in the positions appropriately theirs. Why, then, their evident agony? Because the Fox social structure was not doing anything, save for the clan ceremonies and a few other such activities. Their male need was to find male tasks to do, a whole year's worth of tasks every year, to express their manhood by doing male work, and thereby not merely to occupy those social positions but to *be*—a son, a husband, a father —in short, a man.

7. Community Paralysis and Its Cure

I F Fox social structure had been at work in a full range of
community activity, Fox veterans would probably not have
been building Legion halls—they would have felt themselves to be men already. The various positions of Fox social
structure were present, the men were in these positions, and
after a fashion the structures worked. But Fox structures in
most activities most of the time no longer worked well, and
therefore filling the various positions was not rewarding. The
question became: how had these formal social structures,
which were social devices for getting things done, become
immobilized? Precisely, what was wrong with the Fox
community?

Toward the end of my second summer among the Fox in
1953, the one answer compelling to me began to emerge out

of recent experience and earlier conversations: the Fox community was structurally paralyzed.* "Structural paralysis" is a state of chronic disarticulation in the community–wide webs of influence and authority which form a small community. Fox structural paralysis had been caused and was being sustained by a benevolent, alien government through its pre-emption of responsibilities for the daily details of running community-wide Fox affairs.

In the Fox community, I came to see that all activities fell visibly into either of two sets. For one set, the community, or some part of it, was busily and adequately competent. The young men were mostly in this mood when they were building their American Legion Hall in 1952; most Fox were this way each Sunday during the summer when they held their clan ceremonials; each August the whole community was in this effective mood during the annual Mesquakie Pow-wow, when the Fox acted as hosts to other Indians and to white paying guests. In the second set of activities, such as school affairs, matters of health, and law and order, the community was torn by mutual hostility, fear, ignorance, self-pity, and a feeling of incompetence. In this set of activities, the Fox were structuarally paralyzed.

The two sets did not divide activities that were traditional against others that were new, or fun against work, or sacred against profane. One thing was consistently present in the first category and absent in the second. In the first, the Fox themselves had ultimate responsibility—events would occur only if the Fox as individuals and as a group caused them to occur. In the second, affairs were run by the United States Government or by state and county officials. This contrast suggested to me that structural paralysis, in this context where cultures meet, was caused by outside government—and it

* Among the Chicago students, it was Robert Rietz who most consistently thought in the general directions here reported.

didn't matter critically whether that interference was benevolent or not.

The annual Pow-wow was a large and complex affair. Each year about five hundred out of the six hundred Fox—men, women, and children—participated in some manner. A few thousand non-Fox attended and several thousand dollars were taken in. As Miller had earlier shown, the division of labor among the Fox was necessarily elaborate: dancers and singers, ticket sellers and takers, persons to park cars, announcers, electricians, carpenters, and many more. The preparations began a few weeks in advance; the Pow-wow itself lasted four days; the tidying up and the bookkeeping was not finished until two or three weeks after it was over. The people felt proud and were, during these weeks, demonstrably competent. There were few large and considered changes from one annual Pow-wow to the next; the procedures and the elaborate division of labor seemed to have accrued from countless small innovations over the years. By and large, each man did each year what he did the year before. Still, running the Pow-wow was probably more complex several times over than running the Fox school or the small community health program (assuming of course that professional knowledge—teachers and doctors—could be hired). No outside official ran the Pow-wow.

The running of Fox education stood in remarkable contrast. The Congress of the United States, when it appropriates money for Indian affairs, makes the Secretary of the Interior legally responsible for spending the money well; that responsibility is in turn delegated to an assistant secretary, thence to the commissioner of Indian Affairs, thence down through the hierarchy of the Bureau of Indian Affairs. Ultimately, in the handling of Fox education responsibility for the wise spending of the money (in 1952 approximately $45,000 a year) came to rest with the principal of the federally managed grade school and the superintendent of the nearby white public school system where the Fox children attended junior and senior high school. No responsibility came to rest with a Fox school board or any other Fox organization. Whenever some issue arose having to do with their schools, the Fox were fearful of outsiders and mistrustful of each other; as individuals, they felt unable to judge school matters with self-confidence, and as a group they were unable to arrive at workable community decisions.

You will recall that in 1952 the Bureau of Indian Affairs had decided to transfer eighth grade students from the Fox school to the nearby public school. I came to understand the Fox response to this episode when I realized that in this and other school affairs there was no workable articulation between official Fox leadership, vested in the tribal council, and the Fox community at large, although the council had nominal responsibility and authority in the community. Bureau officials often tried to get the agreement of the tribal council, but community sentiment crystallized, almost impulsively, against any change. The councilmen knew and generally shared the community sentiments; they also knew themselves to be powerless and, for both personal and altruistic reasons, they did not want to alienate the Bureau officials.

It became apparent to me that in such affairs the councilmen equivocated both with the Bureau officials and with members of the community while they attempted to stall, casting about for help from outside white political powers; they were reduced to artful dickering. Bureau officials in turn equivocated and stalled as long as there appeared to be hope that the council might agree. On both sides there was vested interest in ambiguity. In each such episode, therefore, the Fox people could not tell what the councilmen and the government officials were doing, and there was talk of "sellout" as anxiety was turned by Fox against Fox. The proposed change was eventually made without formal council approval, and whatever the council had actually done, they were accused by the Fox of selling out. In such a situation, councilmen could not think about schools, only about dickering and self-preservation; people could not think about schools and could not make reasonable judgments about the competence of councilmen in matters relevant to schools.

There existed, thus, no working web of influence or authority among the Fox in respect to schools, and the same story could be told in respect to Fox health and Fox law and order. Nor, under such conditions, could a web of authority be built by the accretion of habit and experience. In these areas of Fox life, the structural paralysis of the community became apparent. To be politically viable, any human community must array itself as a set of systems of influence and authority to meet particular needs as they arise. The particular channels of influence and the kinds and amounts of coercive authority used may differ among communities, and the traditional Fox system was quite different from our own. For example, the Fox allowed the legitimate use of only very limited amounts of coercion—mother's brothers might discipline their sister's sons, fathers might mildly discipline sons, and the incumbents of a few other social slots might legitimately employ coercion in specific contexts. Traditionally, Fox decisions were made unanimously, in most kinds of situations, or not at all. But traditionally the Fox were a remarkably viable people politically, notoriously so in the eyes of white men and of other Indians who in bygone years had to contend with them.

But the Fox had become structurally paralyzed. How did this come about? I turned again to the history of the Fox, to one feature of that history that newly seemed crucial. The Fox have long been in close contact with the Government of the United States. By the 1860s they had lost their autonomy in foreign affairs; of course this included their power to wage war, and they no longer needed to remain ready for their own defense. This loss of autonomy had a crucial effect: it removed perhaps the clearest and most frequent occasion for the exercise of a community-wide web of influence and authority, through which the Fox could arrive at community-wide judgments. In other aspects of traditional Fox life—matters of economy, training the young, religion, internal order—judgments were usually left to individuals and to various groups within the community acting independently, and questions that required community-wide decisions arose rarely. But in matters of war and peace, the very nature of Fox warfare required that each Fox have a life-and-death interest in the possible actions of every other Fox. War parties often were sent out solely at the initiative of individuals or small groups of warriors. But more typically, these actions required community-wide judgments; small war parties had to be mobilized by community-wide action or, more often, restrained by community-wide action.

To reach such community-wide decisions, the Fox community traditionally sorted itself out by patrilineal clan, with the several clans in turn joined in a council of older men, the heads of the clans. We earlier saw how the chain of relatives within a clan provided a system of roles such that a clan group could arrive with some dispatch at a corporate opinion expressed unanimously. Similarly the older clan heads, joined in council, were so constituted that they usually could reconcile with some dispatch the divergent sentiments of the several clans and reach a common judgment about the matter at hand. Each clan head could thence carry the matter back to his clan in a new form, perhaps compromised, with reconsideration within each clan facilitated by the same chain of grandfather-to-father-to-son relationships. Influence in such a system flowed rather strongly from old to young, but was checked by the patterned alliance between all grandfathers and grandsons that provided assurance that the sentiments of the young would be heard and their interests respected.

It came to this: community-wide decisions as to war and peace were made very largely according to the judgments of the old men; yet the young men upon whom as warriors would fall the work of war were held within the decision-making body, their acquiescence to the decisions almost assured. By such an arangement of themselves the Fox traditionally arrived at their judgments on war and peace. When the more rare community-wide decisions were required in other areas—economic, religious, matters of internal order— the same social machinery stood ready for that work as well. This formal structure had every appearance of pragmatic beauty and effectiveness. But what occurred when Fox autonomy in their foreign affairs was lost?

We know from history, from the studies of social scientists, and from our own experiences that in any society a man gains the capacity to wield influence and authority by earning a reputation with other men for knowledgeable reliability. Two men in identical social positions will enjoy identical nominal authority, but only the man who has earned such a reputation will wield that authority effectively. A working web of influence and authority is a system of reputations that are continually tested and retested in use. Such working relationships among men must be built up over months and years, and they can continue to exist only by frequent use. Formal social structures establish traditional channels and rules for the proper exercise of authority, but the actual web of influence in any community comes to working order and stays in working order only in use.

This knowledge of history and society led me to think again of the father-to-son chain within a hypothetical Fox clan, some generations ago. The youngest, I imagined, twenty years old, was a fledgling warrior, eager for the chance to go on the warpath and thus earn war honors, thus a wife, thus many things Fox men seek. The father of that young man was forty, a seasoned warrior, probably a war leader, knowledgeable and pragmatic in his calculation of the odds of victory or defeat and of alternative strategies. The oldest was sixty, father to the man and grandfather to the young man, long retired from the warpath, an elder, possibly a clan head and a member of the council, who understood the pragmatic calculations of his son, comprehended the frustration of his grandson, knew as well the angers of the women related to Fox men slain earlier but unrevenged and the fears of the women related to the living men who would go out to fight. The three men came to any policy question—and especially one of peace or war—from different positions, with differing knowledge and interest and probably different judgments. But their interests were all real, their opinions all "true." In expressing these interests, one to the other, the men in effect proved each other, proved themselves, discovered and rediscovered each other and themselves.

But when that work was removed, what was left similarly serious and complex for these men to confront, by which each might test the other and himself? Fox men, in 1952 and 1953, sometimes could be heard in dispute or gossip about the heavy drinking of one of them, or about getting a job, or about what was wrong with the school, and so on. But in such matters, who compared to another of his fellows really knew anything more? And who was on the side of whom? The formal structure remained, but the work it once did was no longer there, nor was there new work, which under existing conditions the men in that structure could take up.

Thus I came to see that to the Fox the loss of autonomy in the issues and actions of war and peace meant the weakening, through infrequent use of their community-wide web of influence and authority, and hence the loss of the ability to come quickly to thoughtful and informed community-wide judgments. Much of the traditional social structure, the older and formal configuration of channels and rules, was not destroyed, though some of it (the council of old men, for example) was lost; but the surviving structure was paralyzed through disuse.

After the 1860s there were in Fox life fewer and fewer occasions of any kind when community-wide judgments were required, hence fewer occasions for the re-creation of a web of influence and authority through which such judgments could dependably arise. In the succeeding years, and especially around 1900 the Fox began to experience a particular kind of protective meddling—from a benevolent but powerful alien government. The United States took over from the family and other groups the major responsibilities for education, health, and internal order. In doing so the U.S. government centralized these functions, made them community wide. The aim was benevolent, to keep these "inexperienced" communities from hurting themselves, and so the Bureau of Indian Affairs began to run these newly centralized community functions in all the daily, down-to-earth details.

Perhaps these centralized, year-round, community-wide functions could have provided in time frequent occasions for coming to community judgments, a rough equivalent ot the earlier occasions of peace-and-war. Perhaps they could have been run according to the formal channels established by traditional Fox social structure, or perhaps they would have required new or modified structures; it is no matter, for a people's social structure is never fixed for all time, is always undergoing modification, and there are recorded instances of the most pervasive and radical changes effectively occurring among tribal groups, including some American Indian groups, in a single generation. But this did not occur among the Fox because it was given no chance to occur; matters of education, health, and internal order did not become matters that required Fox community judgments. The Fox community functions were run in all details by outside government, first federal and later state. And no other occasions for community wide judgments arose, excepting the annual Pow-wow.

Thus I came to see that the Fox had become structurally paralyzed in most realms of community life. The formal structures were there, both traditional and new, but in most realms of activity they did not work. Two wedges had been driven among the members of the community, alienating them from one another. First, leaders who had no real power could not but be alienated from the people who chose them; the official leader became a dickerer. Second, blocks of the population could not but form factions chronically opposed to one another. Both wedges were possible because, authority having been pre-empted by a benevolent government, the behavior of the community members had little controlling effect on the work at hand. Men could not become proficient when they could not learn. When the people who selected leadership could not see the relevant effects of the actions of their leaders, they could not thereby judge their compe-tence. Nor would men long or effectively follow the leaders they chose, for there were no tangible rewards for deference to another's judgment. The community had become politi-cally immobilized; it was no longer able to arrive at timely decisions to coordinate community-wide action effectively, no matter how great the sense of need.

It seemed evident: the initial cause of Fox structural pa-ralysis appears to have been the loss of autonomy in foreign affairs. However, *the immediate cause of continued Fox paralysis was the continued pre-emption by outside govern-ment of the responsibility for running all the affairs of Fox life that were community-wide and recurred around the year.*

It was perhaps no wonder that some Fox had been known to comment. "We *like* people to take care of us."

The Pow-wow, however, pointed to the potential for community-wide action that existed immobilized among the Fox. The early traditional web of influence and authority had been kept in working order by the frequent necessity of handling foreign affairs; it had therefore been available for the less frequent community judgments in other areas. The contemporary web of influence and authority that formed around the Pow-wow seemed roughly parallel. The Pow-wow, it was true, rarely required difficult decisions where much was at stake and a diversity of serious opinion had to be resolved, so its strength as a social system was difficult to assess empirically; my impression was of some vulnerability. The potential, however, was clear.

The continuing cause of paralysis was solely the pre-emption by a benevolent government of the responsibility for *running* things—for the daily details of buying chalk and hiring and firing teachers, for example. But *financial* responsibility was a wholly separable matter, a matter of social justice and not Fox social structure that had to be resolved in terms of specific Fox need and the actual limits of Fox income. The money involved was trivial, about $45,000 annually in 1952 and 1953; such an amount could easily have been capitalized in a Fox trust fund. It is not unusual in the United States for national and state governments to appropriate money for local needs but at the same time to give local bodies the authority for spending the money and to hold local officials legally responsible for spending the money for the purposes stipulated. I was not, that is, favoring the much debated policy of "termination" of all federal government responsibilities in Indian affairs. Rather, I was dealing with the unhappy manner in which those responsibilities had been acquitted and with a happier manner in which they could be acquitted.

The Fox community was structurally paralyzed. Structural paralysis could have far-reaching psychological effects in the kind of human society represented by the Fox. The Fox community had been small and autonomous; the community still felt itself to be an autonomous and persisting historical entity and not a dependent part of some larger social order; Fox individuals felt themselves to be first Fox, then (and very abstractly) Americans. But Fox society had to perform work to be tangible; a workable community-wide web of influence and authority, by its exercise in the workaday world, once served that small and autonomous society as a living expression, an acting out and a reaffirmation, of the social order it organized. For such peoples who did not find the concepts of "nation" or "one world" convincing, the absence of such reaffirmation would require psychic defenses, or psychic damage would soon occur. It had become difficult for them to answer to their own satisfaction the crucial question: Who am I?

Thus I came to be pursuaded that a satisfying life in any small and semi-autonomous community requires the systematic arrangement of tasks carried out by men in a coherent system of social positions. A human lifetime in such a society is a movement through those positions, a performance in sequence of those tasks. The meaning of each task is made evident by its coherent place in the large design. Traditionally, being a hunter was meaningful because one's wife and children were not hunters, and because one was once a boy who could not hunt and would become an old man who would not need to hunt.

Pre-eminently, such a society is a moral order. Traditionally, one did not go hunting solely in order to have meat (though that result followed); one went hunting because, at that juncture in his life career, he was a hunter, and hunting was the evident and meaningful and decent thing hunters do. Similarly, in our urban Western life, fathers do not feed sons solely in order that they grow, but because feeding sons is what being a decent father is. In small and autonomous communities generally such webs of moral obligation systematically tie each man to many others and so bind the total group and make of it a morally ordered community. *The capstone of the large design is found in those few tasks the community does, not as a family or clan or war party, but as a single organized unit.* Through recurrent community-wide work, which typically includes religious rituals and political actions, the people enact their group identity and reaffirm their moral order. When the large design cannot be thus reaffirmed its implicit certainty and rightness are gone, being father or husband loses much of its meaning, and all together it becomes less possible to be a man.

But the Fox no longer did recurrent, year-round work in which they acted as a whole society, so the Fox group, that historic and functioning entity, became to the Fox a kind of memory, acted out by the whole group only briefly each year in the Pow-wow.

Structural paralysis of the kind I observed in the Fox appeared to be general among Indians in the United States and Canada. It seemed equally probable that structural paralysis affected a large portion of the small communities of enclaved tribal people and peasants around the world.

Structural paralysis had continued in this Fox community because a benevolent alien government had pre-empted responsibility for running in detail all the important community-wide services. The Fox, unless that pre-emption should stop, would not again compellingly feel themselves to be men. I believed that regaining authority over the running of things was all they needed, to do male tasks and again to feel themselves to be men.

At the beginning of my second summer among the Fox a group of students from Chicago had joined us. All of us, those in the community and others in Chicago, were still trying to do action anthropology, to help while we learned and to learn while we helped. Sadly, the more I came to recognize the underlying nature of the discomfort of this small community, the more my "helping" was reduced to mere talk.

At the end of the summer we left the Fox community, my wife and I—and now, much later, the mere talk that is this book.

8. Notes in the Margin:

Culture as Code

I T IS time, again, to shift from the Fox, to observe in retrospect the observers of the Fox, the writer in particular. What typically goes on in Western heads? The notion of character, it was earlier said, and that double curse, nondescription by the notion of character. These habits of mind went on, and when they did the observers were estranged; they could not relate to the people they saw because they saw too little to relate to. They may have felt pity or contempt or indifference, but underlying all these, they were estranged.

And can one do anything about this? The opposite of being estranged is to find the life of a people believable. The anthropologist Robert Redfield once said that in coming to understand men of another culture one comes to recognize himself in them, himself in another guise. "One comes to recognize himself." That means, of course, that some of the things one sees are pleasant; it also means that one sees, as when he looks into himself, things that are not at all pleasant. The important fact is that one has found a people believable—that one can, given everything he knows about them, imagine himself (neither all god nor all beast) doing whatever they do.

The problem is: What is the nature of that other guise? What devices of mind promise to help in cutting through, and thus to recognize oneself in an alien other, to find that other people believable?

That observer of the Fox, the writer, chanced upon one such device of mind, the notion of *social structure*. A further device, the notion of *world view*, came into play more briefly. One may attempt now to look at these devices to discover the kinds of selective observation they impose and the kinds of arrangements of selected items they dictate, the work they can be made to do. A final device must later be briefly mentioned: the notion of *personality*.

There is not much esoteric mystery in these notions. In everyday life in familiar surroundings, all normal men competently take up, unawares, first one and then another of these devices of mind. But in encounters across cultural boundaries, Western minds seem to freeze, to lose their normal agility. Thus it seems necessary to isolate these commonplace devices, to name them, bring them to full consciousness, make them thereby deployable. One hopes thus to gain by exercise of will, in confronting the life of an alien people, that normal agility which comes unbidden in more familiar contexts. Alien lives are believable; to the degree that they seem otherwise the mind cozens itself. The remedy is to grope toward a measure of self-awareness about and deliberate self-control over the everyday workings of the mind.

That is what cultural anthropology has been and still is: such a groping.

Culture Is Code

An observer went to the Fox. As a result some artifacts exist, descriptions of the Fox shaped by the devices at hand. We turn now to watch those devices behaving, to see them doing the work they can do. The device "social structure" selectively describes the life of a people as an enduring organization of positions in and out of which men move; description of the Fox was shaped by this device in Chapter 4 ("The Big Impossible") and more self-consciously in Chapters 6 and 7 ("Fox Social Structure" and "Community Paralysis"). The device of "world view" describes a people by depicting their perception of the nature of men and things as they perceive that universe; early description of the Fox as "harmonious" in Chapter 3 was shaped by this device, in some distortion.

Each of these mental devices selects different phenomena and puts in different order the phenomena selected, thus differently to describe some part of an alien life. Both of them, however, make three large selections from among the facts which are that alien life. *First*, both put to one side the fact that people create material products—tools, weapons, clothing and shelter, objects of art, and so on. The minds of observers do typically pause over such products, and curiosity about them is unmistakably reflected in museums, but men are not often moved or disturbed. Techniques of manufacture may puzzle, a strange art style may puzzle most profoundly, but most men most of the time are not made uncomfortable by them, and description guided by the devices of social structure and world view pass by these possible reflections of Fox life. Neither of these devices attempts to see the Fox by looking at their products, though that would always be possible. In contrast, the everyday actions of alien men not only puzzle but often disturb, and both of these mental devices attempt to come to grips with such Fox activity.

Second, both of these devices reject certain conventional Western categories of human action. When a man looks at the life of an alien people, he does not see merely an array of actions independent of each other; rather, that alien life comes to his mind most directly as whole sets of actions joined by their focus on some conspicuous goal or goals. Most immediately, one would see that the Fox at this moment are "having a clan feast," or that this Fox family is now "eating dinner," and so on—events large and small unfolding in a sequence. But the Western tradition has the received notion that there exist certain more or less self-evident large categories into which these events fall, categories labeled by such words as economics, politics, religion, education, and leisure. A clan feast and a family meal, it seems evident, are both economic events, since goods are being consumed; the clan feast is in addition a religious event but the meal is not: neither appears to be a political event; and so on.

Westerners as they live their lives think and act in terms of such categories, and much of social science reflects this fact: the West has developed the study of economics, politics and law, comparative religion, education, etc. (Too consistently to be mere accident, fun is ignored as a subject of study.) All those Western (or Western-derived) disciplines, often in principle and always in fact, move from the notion that among all possible events some for example are economic, and these economic events can usefully be selected for study. Some economists say that economics is the study of "economizing" and that their discipline therefore includes for study all the choices men must make, which is to say that every human event is economic; but, in reality, if money changes hands (or if numbers move on the ledger) an event gets included in economic studies, and if money does not change hands the event usually is not included.

In contrast, the two devices of mind we here entertain attempt no such selection and classification among events; they leave events unsorted in respect to such categories as economic, political, and so on. Social structure describes the way a people order themselves in *any* event and summarizes the various orderings of *all* events in the life of that people. The notion of world view similarly is concerned with some aspect of *every* event in a Fox year or lifetime.

Third, the two devices do another most critical thing: they describe not behavior itself but ideas shared in the heads of a people about behavior—in a word, aspects of the *culture* of that people.

Suppose a man, somewhere at some moment, makes his facial expression become blank. That act may in one instance be included in description shaped by both the devices before us, and in another instance it will be included by neither of these devices. A raised eyebrow, or a relaxed muscular tone, or a stroll through a field, any single instance of all these may or may not be included. What makes the difference is whether these actions are *publicly meaningful* to the actors. Not all behavior is publicly meaningful and any given act may be so on one occasion and not on another. Breathing at a normal rate usually goes unnoticed; fast breathing on certain occasions may be recognized as an expression of anger or passion and thereby be publicly meaningful; when breathing stops that is always publicly meaningful—indeed, the individual becomes a new social entity, an ancestor, perhaps. So one does not, guided by the two devices before us, simply watch actions or even patterns of recurrent actions. One watches actions and reactions, especially reactions. Acts that evoke reactions are publicly meaningful. In description shaped by the two devices these are included; an infinite number of other acts are left to one side.

Imagine three Fox men. The first shouts at a second; this could mean a virtual infinity of things. The second in turn braces himself in anger; this could still mean many things. But the third Fox, a bystander not directly involved, registers moral shock and perhaps gossips later about the outrage. The behavior of the third party relative to the other two is most directly revealing of the shared ideas in the heads of that people about the behavior in question. In small communities the whole community comes close to being a third party to most interaction; and a small community carries on, quite literally, a running everyday commentary, the content of which is assessment of men's behavior by the standards of their shared ideas, their culture. This commentary has been likened to the chorus in classic Greek drama, which observes the protagonists, which deeply comprehends and comments on the actions in concert.

The culture of a small community is the code the people carry in common in their heads as to (among other things) how men of the community ought to behave. Culture is code. The devices of social structure and world view attend, not behavior directly, but shared codes about behavior—in a word, aspects of culture.

In sum: the two devices cause description to focus on behavior, not material products; they focus on aspects of behavior to be found in any and all events; and they select only publicly meaningful behavior and elicit aspects of the shared codes which provide that meaning, aspects of the culture of the community under view. But in other respects these devices are markedly different.

Social Structure

Description of the Fox shaped by the notion of social structure is one artifact, put down earlier in Chapter 6. There description moves first from one event, a clan feast; any event could be chosen, arbitrarily. That event parades many actions and reactions, a welter of publicly meaningful behavior. But the notion of social structure, like all descriptive notions, selects peculiarly and orders that selected information peculiarly. Of all the behavior paraded, the Fox actions that receive attention are those revealing that an individual Fox is thought by his fellows to occupy at this moment a certain social slot, a publicly acknowledged social identity, and in virtue of that occupancy is expected to behave in certain publicly acknowledged ways. In other words, observation is attuned to recurrent patterns of action and approving or disapproving reaction, and especially, observation is attuned to the reactions of third parties. Assisted further by questioning the actors, one asks: "Why that action?" or "Why that approval?" The answer might be "He's stupid" or, "He's the clan head" and only the latter is, in a description of Fox social structure, a datum. It identifies a social slot deemed by Fox to exist and a corresponding pattern of the occupant's behavior expected or preferred by Fox.

In short, description by the notion of social structure is mainly attentive to the identity question: Who is he? The word "person" stems from the Latin *persona*, which meant a mask used by an actor. The word is often narrowly used in anthropology to mean a publicly recognized social slot: Pete Bear is, during a clan feast, a certain person, a clan head; on other occasions Pete Bear is other persons: a house head or a member of the Pow-wow committee, for example. The word "role" is often used to denote the corresponding pattern of publicly expected behavior: Bear, being the person, "clan head," acts out the appropriate role (or fails to). The analogy to the stage is obvious and intended. Thus, by the notion of social structure, a double aspect of each and any event, and ideally of all events, is selected: out of the full complexity of an event, description shaped by the notion has sifted out persons and roles—who each actor is publicly imagined to be, and how, being that, he is expected to behave publicly.

The descriptive notion of social structure also dictates a peculiar arrangement of these selected items of information. Ideally, description of the clan feast has come to identify all the persons and roles imagined by the Fox to operate there, and moving through a series of similar Fox events, description comes to identify the full array of persons and roles which are the building blocks of Fox social structure. These would read like a laundry list if description stopped here. What arrangement of these items of information are then dictated by the notion?

One thinkable arrangement has already gone by the board and, by strict adherence to the notion of social structure, would be unrecoverable. Description has let go of individual Fox men; these selected items of information could not be sorted according to individual Fox actors. Pete Bear, deemed by his fellows to be clan head, behaves in a fashion that, so far as the reactions of his fellows reveal, is expectable; and on other occasions other Fox, deemed by their fellows to be clan heads, behave similarly. These data have, as it were, gone into a box marked "clan head." The same Pete Bear on other occasions is deemed by his fellows "grandfather" and "old man" and "mother's brother" and "a Fox" (in respect to non-Fox), etc., and those data are dispersed into similar boxes. Description by the notion of social structure selectively attends to the question "Who is this man, that behaves in this way?" only in terms of social identities. It does not matter which individual Fox acts, only that he is deemed clan head, etc. Thus one could no longer disentangle Pete Bear's clan head behaviors from the clanhead behavior of other Fox, nor could one find and assemble the many behaviors of Pete Bear as grandfather, old man, mother's brother, etc.

Thus description guided by the notion of social structure is left with such figurative boxes of items, each labeled with the name of some social slot (some person) imagined by the Fox to exist. How are those data to be arranged, one box of such items with another?

First, by pairs of such social slots that are related to each other. The "clan heads" at clan feasts relate in specific ways to any Fox who is a member of a guest clan. And "clan heads" relate at feasts in specific ways to "fellow clansmen"; but in turn "fellow clansmen" relationships break down into a battery of other paired relationships: clan head is "grandfather" to some fellow clansmen, "father" to others, "brother" to still others, thinkably (though improbably) "son" to some ancient of the tribe. Thus a set of paired social slots can be arranged, with the specific content of each relationship provided by corresponding expectations about conduct, about roles. Second, these pairs form chains of paired relationships, as in the chain of grandfather to father to son, and by further extension these chains form a complex system of relationhips. Thus description comes to reveal how, when the total Fox population is gathered for a clan feast, labor can be divided and goods and authority can flow in specified ways, and how over longer stretches of time, knowledge can flow non–randomly as well. All this by those ideas in Fox heads about persons and roles, facts elicited and then arranged by the notion of social structure.

The phrase "structural pose" is a useful label for any one such arrangement of a total community. During a year, a series of events unfold in the Fox community. At any moment the Fox population is occupied with a particular event, so at any moment the Fox think of themselves as organized by the appropriate arrangement, some one structural pose. In Chapter 6 the structural pose for clan feasts is partly described. Those pages briefly suggest also the unsystematic, unarticulated structural pose for contemporary councils. Elsewhere the Pow-wow is partly described, another pose. And during most hours of the year the Fox are sorted as households operating independently at their several tasks, another pose. So Fox social structure is a series of structural poses, several arrangements of the total community, each of which appears and reappears during the year according to the tasks at hand.

The language in Chapter 6 and in other pages on Fox social structure is frequently inexact. There it is said, in effect, "Host clansmen fast, and guest clansmen eat." More exactly, those sentences should read: "All Fox expect of a particular Fox, who is at this moment a host clansmen, that he fast. . . ." Some host clansmen may not even attend his clan feast. But those pages slipped into the less tiresome language of actual conduct, on the assumption that most men, most of the time, do in fact conform to expectations.

Social structure thus describes one kind of public code in Fox heads, one aspect of the culture of that people.

World View

In earlier chapters, in the context of Fox notions about their natural environment (the History, the buffalo head ceremony, notions about harmony generally), another aspect of

Fox culture is briefly encountered: items from a Fox view of the nature of the universe of men, gods, and things—from the Fox world view.

There could not occur in any small society any event in which the actors did not see themselves as occupants of a publicly acknowledged social position. Similarly, there could not occur any event in which the actors did not share ideas about the nature of the men and things involved. Thus the notion of world view, like the notion of social structure, sifts out a public code that is carried in the heads of a people, that is taken by men to their everyday encounters and thus affects how these men behave.

Alien social structures have been studied with much success; alien world views with less. The reason is clear: the subject matter of a world view is incomparably more difficult. A people's world view is intimately bound up with their language, and the grammar of their language sets the pattern for, and may even delimit, their thought; this appears to be equally true of all languages, Mesquakie (the language of the Fox) and English alike. Grammars help establish categories of habitual thought and seem to establish the very logic by which one thought can follow upon another. Only certain kinds of linguists and cognitive psychologists can move with any measure of sureness in this difficult realm. Surface reflections of its complexity can, however, be recognized if not quite understood.

Western men look out upon an impersonal universe that moves in lawful regularity. To a Western man, a runaway car rolls down the street because of a chain of impersonal causes. A man walks along the street and that too, if much less perfectly, seems to a Westerner to be explained in terms of a chain of causes. If the man is hit by the car, two sets of causes have happened to intersect, and Western men have the notion of accident—random chance—to describe that coincidence.

In contrast, the Fox world is personal. Fox know about causes, but many or even all the acting parts in a chain of causes are, in traditional Fox thought, imbued with "powers," which are not impersonal forces and more closely resemble the Western notions of "wills" and "abilities." And since causes are thus personalized, there need not be and possibly cannot be, in Fox logic, such a thing as an accident. The rolling car, the walking man, and the coincidence of the two, all are explained by some interplay of power or some contention among powers.

More generally: the world view of any people includes a set of ideas about the constitution of man, of nature, and of the supernatural (though not necessarily grouped into these categories), and how, within all this, one item can affect another. Nature may to a people include a wider range of things than Westerners would expect, as might the supernatural, and the constitution ascribed to each category may differ greatly. But by experience universal to men in societies, every world view must evidently include all three—with modern, highly contrived atheistic views being a possible but quite ambiguous exception.

The fascination of inquiry into this subject is obvious. The main difficulties in studying world views do not lie in finding and reporting discrete items of alien belief; rather, they lie in trying to understand the systematic arrangement of a people's traditional thought and in imposing a scheme that seems to fit the facts. An unusual Fox, one with philosophic bent, might talk in abstract terms about cars rolling and men getting hit as the interplay of powers, but an average Fox is more likely to say more simply, "He was witched." In any society, including societies as small as the Fox, a few men are by nature thinkers, prone to thoughtful speculation, but most are not.

Among any people systematic arrangements of ideas about

the world are arrived at and held in mind by thinkers, and men who are not prone to speculation tend to hold to traditional ideas piecemeal, logically unordered, in an unconnected welter of many parts. Among Western scientists, only a few can study meaningfully the world views of alien thinkers. The rest of us can, if we wish, do some part of the less demanding work: we can settle for locating and describing items from that welter, pieces of the alien world view of the average man in his society.

Description shaped by the notion of world view selects an aspect of any and all events in a small community. Entering any such event, affecting men's behavior, is a set of shared ideas about the nature of men, gods, and things. The notion of world view is directed toward a people's cognitive mapping. Ideally, it causes the observer to be attentive (as before) to actions and reactions, this time to discern the cognitive mappings that affect behavior. It is, however, evident that here the observer is very largely dependent on testimony, on the running, natural commentary of the community and in largest part on the special commentary directed toward the observer himself. One depends hugely on the generous impulses of the people that make them want to explain, and on one's capacities to listen well.

Social Structure and World View

Descriptions guided by the notions of social structure and of world view start from opposite corners, as it were, of a people's culture, and they seem to run separate courses. Social structure requires asking of any actor: Who is he? What person is this actor imagined to be? Thence description by social structure seeks corresponding role expectations. World view requires asking of the items of a people's universe of men, gods, and things: What is the nature of these items, as their nature is by these people envisaged?

However, the two modes of description may not be kept wholly separate, nor need they be. In that early brief description of Fox notions about the universe, one finds, dimly, a Fox vision of an array of enduring parts—men, land, supernatural power, the Fox—bound in a harmonious equilibrium. But only a slight translation, a reading on the opposite side as it were, is required to see in this vision indications as to how an average Fox man would typically behave. It seems but a small step to infer from Fox assertions about the nature of things other assertions about how a Fox decently behaves toward those things. Thus, description moves easily from a description by the notion of world view to Fox rules about right conduct, which is to say, to some components of Fox roles required of (unspecified) Fox persons, which is further to say, to some unanticipated features of Fox social structure. Fox notions about a harmony of parts include among those parts the Fox themselves, and thus include a host of rules about conduct between men and men, earlier described as the "circumspect" behavior of the Fox. This, of course, is the very stuff of Fox social structure.

In short, many particular directives for right conduct appear to be simple inference from views about nature. Anciently, the hunter apologized to the bear. Today, somewhat less a matter of direct inference, men leave the fencerows of plowed fields wide and their corners rounded. Still less direct, men then and now avoid an open clash with their fellows, as if such clashes would disturb the universal harmony among men, personalized nature, and the gods. Description by world view assists description by social structure.

The reverse is also true. A description of a people's social structure helps identify many of their ideas about the nature of things and can lead to a gross outline at least of their view of men, nature, and the gods. Fox social structure is a series of structural poses, which reappear each in its turn in the series of Fox events that unfold through the year, and in each of them the Fox view nature as a harmony. That Fox view of the universe does not change from one structural pose to the next; though of course it must be brought concretely to Fox minds more in certain poses (such as clan feasts) than in others (such as tribal council dickerings with white men). And insofar as Fox men are caused in some of the structural positions they hold to call to mind traditional ideas about the general qualities of nature, these ideas will frequently be expressed by them in just those contexts—expressed piecemeal and without concern for any overall scheme of ideas, perhaps, but none the less influential in guiding their actions and our understanding of them.

The two devices of mind, social structure and world view, thus start separately and seem at first to run separate courses, but they come ultimately to overlap. Which is to say: all such devices are mental tools and the resulting descriptions are mental artifacts. As tools, the devices serve to select from the phenomenal world and put in order a small bit, big enough to make some sense and little enough to allow the senses and mind to grasp it. If ultimately these two devices seem to merge, the observer need not feel cheated. They were not invented or logically engineered, they just grew out of our need for coping with the world in some comfort.

Ethos, Parenthetically

Ruth Benedict said, "The Zuni are Apollonian." In poor imitation, the writer observed the Fox and reported, "The Fox are generous, circumspect, and harmonious." This report moved by the notion of character, thus described Fox life as patterns of consistent behavior by an imaginary Fox. Such description is, as earlier noted, treacherously opaque.

But that description could have been narrowed and thereby rendered less opaque. One could put down in those pages not what most Fox do (whether out of habit, moral persuasion, neurosis, or whatever), but something of what Fox think Fox ought to do, the pervading Fox rules about decent conduct. This is description shaped by the notion of *ethos*, description of the conspicuously pervasive aspects of a people's moral code.

Description of a people's life by the notion of ethos can be either of two things. It may be an intuitive sense of central tendencies among the full battery of roles in a community; as such it is a device to make do until more adequate information —i.e., description by the notion of social structure—is at hand. Or it may be a summary statement of central tendencies among roles, a summary derived from a description by the notion of social structure that is already in hand. As such it is a device to sum up large blocks of information that would otherwise be left dispersed.

The notion of ethos, however, uniquely selects and arrays information. From the stuff of social structure, ethos leaves aside social identities (persons) and sifts out only rules for conduct (roles). From all role information, it further sifts out that which has moral connotation to the people, an array of items that are morally imperative.

This leaves little option about arranging the data. The notion of ethos dictates that the selected roles be arrayed, figuratively, in piles as to general kind: for example, for the Fox we would have stacks of rules about generosity, about circumspection, and about harmony. For any particular people, the largest piles of rules, of course, are the ones that serve best to summarize their life.

But there is an option in making these categories of roles. In the earlier descriptions of Fox life the categories of "generosity" and "circumspection" were drawn from the Western cultural tradition. In contrast, "harmony" came out of Fox testimony, out of hearing a Fox version of Fox history and the content of a Fox ceremony. The mix was irrational, since harmony seemed to subsume circumspection and possibly generosity as well. The option appears to be one or the other kind of category, the observer's or the people's, but not both. Precisely how an observer is to discover a category real to an alien people is, by the notion of ethos, not clear; if guided only by that notion, one listens well and hopes for the best.

Finally, when the piles of roles are assembled the notion of ethos permits (though it does not dictate) that the categories be arranged according to some logical hierarchy of principles, more inclusive principles subsuming lesser principles according to the logic of the observer or, thinkably, of the people themselves. The ultimate step in such an enterprise is the generation of a single overarching principle, almost certainly of the observer's making or application. "The Zuni are Apollonian" in the vision of Ruth Benedict, not the Zuni.

Description by the notion of ethos is a poor cousin to description by the notions of social structure and world view. Its beauty is the terse summing-up it yields of the complex life of a people. But ethos describes nothing not described more elegantly by the notion of social structure, when bolstered by the notion of world view. Ethos leaves persons unspecified; social structure does not. Ethos focuses on a few central tendencies; social structure does not. Ethos describes the moral order of a people as a few moral themes; social structure describes that moral order in something of its full complexity and thereby reveals its functional nature. Ethos makes a people seem to be single-minded automatons; social structure makes them seem to be geniuses.

It is doubtful if in small-scale tribal communities (peasant villages may be ambiguous in this respect) there exist any roles about right conduct that are not specific to the incumbents of particular social slots. Rules that dictate circumspect conduct seem usually pervasive in Fox life, but a Fox mother's brother is not expected to be always circumspect toward his sister's son; in certain situations he is expected to be a disciplinarian and a bogeyman. A father is not always circumspect toward an errant son but may scold and cause the son to fast. These proper actions do not detract from the reputations of these men, do not adversely affect public assessment of them. Quite the reverse. These "exceptions" have reasons for being. The notion of social structure keeps such "exceptions" in focus, and allows one to recognize the reasons for their being. The notion of ethos does neither. Terse summary, however, has its own beauty and utility.

Other Matters, Briefly Named

These brief pages on the Fox, leaving aside the observations by their neighbors and most of my early stumbling, in fact contain not two kinds of study (social structure and world view) but a good many. We are concerned to find ways that, by self-conscious exercise of will, the mind looking at an alien world can be made to regain the agility it normally enjoys unawares in familiar contexts. At levels other than the dictates of the two descriptive notions just reviewed, descriptions in these pages have moved haphazardly. Let us briefly review some alternatives.

A tribal or peasant community can be described as if it were isolated and self-contained or as if it were a community enclaved within or subsumed by a larger community. Both are in some sense factual, and certain good purposes can be served by either mode. These pages on the Fox contain description shaped by both images; observation moved back and forth, unawares.

Such a community can also be described as if its life were in a condition of equilibrium or as if it were changing. Again, both are always factually true, and description can move by either mode to good purpose. In these pages, description moves between the two images in partial unawareness.

Finally, one can describe a community as if from the outside or as if through the eyes of the members of that community, from inside—and both to good purposes. In these pages on the Fox, this matter on occasion becomes a point of explicit difficulty, but elsewhere description moves between the two unawares.

All these pairs are independent of each other and of our two descriptive notions, and any combination of pairs is possible, making many different kinds of study. The point is this. The phenomenal world is unsteady enough; devices of mind help hold that world a bit steady; the steadier the devices, the steadier the world, and the clearer is the resulting image of that world.

Guises

We have come full circle. I started my stay among the Fox by hearing others describe a kind of man, and I myself attempted to say something about a Fox kind of man. Perhaps that appears to have been left far behind, but it is not quite so. Following the dictates of the notions of social structure and world view, one would still describe a kind of man, though very differently than before. Now the person who emerges is a hypothetical man with a set of codes in his mind; he is identified with a culture.

Estrangement is common, its opposite more rare. When one hits upon an appropriate mental device, he is able to see better across a cultural boundary, and when one sees well, he must often describe how very different those people are. It is a paradox: the more one takes seriously the fact that people are really very different in culture, the more one comes to recognize, in and behind the differences, the familiar, the universally human.

When the white men of Tama measured the Fox by their list of Western virtues, they in effect denied that the Fox might be culturally different—that the Fox might, for example, think about decent conduct in unfamiliar categories and terms. And denying that the Fox were different, these neighbors looked and in fact found the Fox to appear in some respects very, very different—"unambitious," men quite without motivation, in a word (if one pauses to think) inhuman. Conversely, when one deliberately takes up a device of mind that will do real work, one is likely to find important cultural differences, quite new categories of thought and value. And once these very great differences are seen with some clarity, the Fox come to seem humanly familiar. Out of apparent and almost inhuman lack of motivation there emerges a recognizably human sense of accomplishment, the sense any man would feel if he saw himself, as the Fox do, in a world of eternally balanced harmony among men, nature, and the supernatural.

"One comes to recognize himself in another guise." That guise is of course the codes, the cultures, carried in the heads of men to their encounters, there affecting their behaviors. When one elicits the codes one sees through them the man, the universally human, oneself. The face of the Fox is your own.

Personality

One can in these ways describe a people's life, but only after a fashion. Culture is not behavior; it is an artifact derived from devices that describe how men think or evaluate, not necessarily how men act. Indeed, culture describes only that much of their thought which is shared, publicly meaningful. But knowledge of the culture of a people is quite enough to permit one to live and work effectively, and in some comfort, among them. A Fox man at some particular moment knows that other Fox share with him the notion that at this moment he ought to be a certain person and ought to perform appropriately the corresponding role; and he knows that if he does so, the audience will express approval in certain ways and if he does not, they will express disapproval. In a small, face-to-face group that is relatively little enmeshed in industrialized, city-based styles of living, there is characteristically great homogeneity of mind in respect to these public understandings. If an observer knows this much, knows the culture of the people, he understands a great deal of the life of the place.

Human curiosity necessarily causes one to want to know more—to understand enough to predict whether a particular Fox will or will not take up and act out some person-and-role that his fellows recommend to him, and if so, whether he will do so happily or with some reluctance. The Fox recommend to all males that when they reach their later years, say age fifty, they become clan elders and act accordingly; one would like to understand enough to predict that Pete Bear will in fact accept these recommendations or reject them. One wants to comprehend the psychic economy of that individual man. Or, perhaps in more realistically do-able terms, one wants to comprehend something of the average or basic personality of that people, one wants to predict that of all Fox men to whom a particular person-and-role is recommended, some known per cent will take up that person and adequately act out that role. Such understandings require, in addition to correct description of Fox culture, a very different kind of inquiry in terms of the notion of personality.

Culture is any man's knowledge about how his fellows think and what they expect of him. In studies of personality, culture is like an environment through which human organisms move as they are born, mature, age, and finally die. Culture so seen shapes the experiences of men—dramatically reduces the variety and markedly affects the frequency of particular experiences—and thus helps to determine the configurations of psychic needs and tendencies in those men. And culture so seen presents the occasions which permit or frustrate the expression of the created psychic needs. Cultures, that is, create contours of "input" into human psyches and help shape channels of "output" from those psyches.

My descriptions of Fox life have but fleetingly and implicitly, even accidentally, touched on the notion of personality. Circumspect conduct, as I described it, was at bottom a set of Fox notions about right and wrong. A description of the same features of Fox life in terms of personality would attempt to specify a trait that might be called "timidity" in the usual Fox man, would describe how that timidity got there, and would describe how that timidity helps cause the man frequently to behave circumspectly. Such a description of Fox life would describe how many Fox men become timid, how a few become aggressive, and how, knowing that circumspect conduct is right conduct, both timid men and agressive men differently manage to behave circumspectly or fail to.

The difference between a description in terms of culture and one in terms of personality is at bottom a difference not

in the facts employed but in the way the facts are arrayed—
a difference in the way facts are placed next to each other so
as to permit inference. Personality description does, it is true,
include new kinds of facts—blood chemistry, perhaps, and, to
our immediate purpose, behavior not deemed (by that
people) publicly meaningful, such as meaningless change in
rate of breathing. But like cultural study, personality study
takes up and in the main depends upon all publicly meaningful behavior. Thus, because both move from the same information, the difference between these two descriptions of a
life is elusive and may seem merely a matter of saying the
same thing twice in different words.

In cultural description one sees a Fox act and others react
in a way suggesting that, in the judgment of that people,
grandfathers ought not boss grandsons; then one sees another
man act and others react in a way suggesting the same thing;
these two observations are placed together by the mind and
upon an accumulation of such instances the shared Fox notion
becomes evident: grandfathers do not in decency boss grandsons. The mind, guided by the notion of social structure (or
world view or, in blanket terms, culture) has let go of, has
never really attended, the particular men who act. In contrast,
one cannot when guided by the notion of personality so
quickly ignore the particular men. It begins to matter that
this grandfather who patiently nurtures his grandson is also
father to a son nearby and can boss him, and it matters that
another Fox grandfather has no nearby son. It matters equally
that one grandfather grew up in the security of a large circle
of relatives including supportive grandfathers, and the other
did not; and it matters, cumulatively, that many Fox grandfathers are in these respects like the first and only a few like
the second.

In personality study, then, facts are arrayed along an axis of
life career, along the sequence of experiences of one individual

(or several similar individuals) from birth to death, which sequence "puts in" and "takes out" desires, tensions, what not. Responses to inkblots do not of themselves reveal personality, and observations of actions and reactions do not of themselves reveal culture. These are only data. Both reveal personality and both reveal culture, and the essential difference is the way aggregates of the data are arrayed.

The life of a people can, after a fashion, be described by describing their culture. But the description of culture is only a way station toward a description in terms of personality, and only the latter can reach very close to the real goal, a self-satisfying description of the behavior which unfolds in that place. It need not be added that no man has ever achieved that remotely possible result.

9. *Postscript:* **The Fox View of the Fox Self**

S OMETIME IN the midst of the instructive activities of the Fox veterans, I had become much less aware of any estrangement from the Fox, much more confident that the life of this community was to me coming to be believable. In the ensuing reading and observation into Fox social structure and its paralysis, Fox life came to seem to me quite believable. But had it?

We left the Fox, my wife and I, to return to Chicago in September, 1953. Some while after, it came one day to mind (I cannot recall in what context) how very flat my memories were of those Fox men we had known so long. I could recall, for example, much of the kind of man Bill Walker was— Walker, the unusually effective sometime chairman of the Legion; but I could not suppose he had always been precisely the kind of man I knew, and I had no sense of how he got that way. Perhaps he was patient and gentle from infancy, an inheritor of unusual genes or born of an unusual womb, and so came into adulthood temperamentally fitted for the demands of Fox leadership. Or perhaps he had spent a more boisterous youth, had gone away to government Indian schools, had returned (as many have) hell bent on shaping his people up, had received stern reprimands from his father and effective supportive advice from his grandfather, and had himself been shaped. Or maybe large disappointments or tragedies were his teachers. Even the man I knew was in certain respects obscure. Perhaps leadership positions were critical to him and he was miserable without such work. Or perhaps it really was (as he had in any event to pretend) a matter of indifference to him; he was able and willing if asked, content not to be asked.

Among these, I could not and cannot now choose. Why do I not know these things? A part of the answer is obvious: I did not do a personality study, nor did I ever map out and do the kind of cultural study that moves halfway toward a personality study, the collection of life histories. But that answer is hardly sufficient. I did not at the outset plan to do a study of social structure either, but aspects of such a study nevertheless got done. We were "doing" action anthropology, which in total effect means being very nondirective about the abstract kinds of data we would at any moment be seeking; we took occasions to help as they came and similarly took occasions to learn as they came, for (in principle and largely in fact) these were the same occasions. I cannot suppose that my mind was at any moment less ready to recognize and retain a segment from a life history than it was to recognize one or another dimension of social structure. Rather, it is necessary to suppose that I know so little about the personal history of Bill Walker for the simple reason that, in all our associations during those fifteen months, allusions to that information just did not come up. Bill and I talked together for many hours, but his mind did not move, of itself, in these directions. We talked a great deal about the Fox as an enduring people, with a history, a present shape, and perhaps a future. We talked not at all about the unique history, present shape, and destiny of Bill Walker, or of any other particular Fox.

Indeed, there could not have been any strong resistance on my part, because, looking back over parts of this study, it is evident that unknowingly and without adequate information I did consider personality, here and there. George Marlin was dragged through cycles of pro- and anti-Fox mood; if there is any plausibility in that account, it cannot derive from a description of social structure alone. Rather, Fox social structure became for that purpose an environment that the psyche of George Marlin handled in a tragic and conspicuous way. And the central meaning I derived from building the Legion hall required, for the plausibility that meaning might contain, a population of psyches which "needed" an environment of persons and roles, an environment of publicly named social slots to move into and publicly evaluated things to do in those social places. The larger, parallel argument that the Fox community was structurally paralyzed required similarly such a population of Fox psyches.

The information did not "come in," I believe, because in all my associations in the community it was not offered. Others, it should be noted, have caused Indian minds to run in these directions, so that we now possess several quite good autobiographies of Indians. I do not know how difficult or easy those other anthropologists found their task. Ruth Underhill, the anthropologist who recorded and put in order *Autobiography of a Papago Woman*, reported that Chona, whose life story is told, simply reminisced, that the account as it came from her lips over weeks or months was unusually scrambled in chronology. I recall in those pages no instance where Chona suggests a sense of events shaping her, or a sense that she acted because of some acquired shape, though it is quite obvious to the reader that such was often the case.

Thus, the images I hold of Bill Walker and the other Fox are all alike: timeless, surface states of being, inferred from the actions visible to me. Large unknowns remain: the shaping events in a man's past, and most of the less obvious personal needs of his present. Such information was not offered by the Fox, about themselves or about fellow Fox. The question is: why?

To a member of mobile, city-bred, modern Western society, everyday life in one's home community is composed largely of relatively brief encounters with strangers. Most of our work is done with virtual strangers, as is a great deal of our play and worship. To a Western mind, an encounter with a stranger-become-acquaintance seems an encounter between two egos: I come bringing myself and my personal history; I invest some part of myself in the encounter; I go away carrying my modified self to some other similar meeting. The reality of the encounter is not that I am student and he professor, or I nephew and he uncle, or that I am English-derived American and he Fox-American, though these thoughts are present, importantly affecting how we act. But with these, overriding them often, seeming more tangible, certain, and right, a Western mind senses: I have met him and he me.

Perhaps it is inevitably thus, when societies become highly industrialized and mobile and the rate of social change becomes rapid, upsetting traditional roles. Rapid change makes the expectations of any role more ambiguous, making old roles obsolete and forever bringing new ones into being. And all the while, men have to get on with their work, which means anticipating with some accuracy the actions of their fellows. Perhaps, in such situations, men must inevitably place less reliance on knowing another's changeable social position and must think more of personality, of the more enduring features of the unique individuals they encounter.

But there are peoples in the world to whom the notion of "personality" is less useful in everyday life; the notion does not come easily or often to their minds. To such peoples, the very idea of personality is cumbersome and awkward, or even meaningless. The Fox, I think, and the American Indians generally, are such peoples; perhaps tribal peoples in general are.

Perhaps the Fox do not often think of the human psyche as having enduring traits; but saying this names something the Fox are not, indicates ideas they do not have, and we have agreed such a statement is not helpful. How *do* they think about the human psyche? Considering this problem, I come to deal again, in retrospect, with the Fox view of the world, with the unwritten Fox notions about the nature of the universe of men and things. That view holds the land to be "thou," not "it." Necessarily it must also assert notions about the nature of the human psyche, some Fox view of the Fox self.

The human species lives only in groups, and all these groups are organized. It follows that two very different things are true about humans-in-groups. Any human group is made up of organisms; these are born, live some while, assume a shape and mental profile in virtue of their genes and experience, and die. Such a group is also made up of an enduring system of organization; particular people move into and out of sundry social slots, but the slots tend to remain. No normal man in any society can be oblivious to either of these facts, in the concrete particulars in which they impinge on his experience.

But human cultures are able drastically to mold experience, to draw one dimension of reality into sharp relief and suppress another. Our contemporary Western life draws into sharpest focus the birth and continuing flow of experience and the resulting personal qualities of mind of individual human organisms; when we meet another we want to know where he has been, what he has done, what kind of man he has become, and where he seems to be going. As for that other dimension of reality, enduring organization, we of course must continuously act in its terms and are therefore aware of it at some level of mental activity. We think often, for example, of those aspects of organization that affect and express ranked status. But it seems that we rarely think about enduring organization with clarity and direction and completeness, except under special circumstances (as when we are required to describe the table of organization of a factory). To appear to think consistently in everyday life about one's social positions and the positions of one's fellows seems, to us, a little indecent.

For the Fox, the emphasis appears to be reversed. The primary reality habitually considered with full awareness by a Fox, somewhat systematically and with clarity and direction, is enduring organization. A Fox, I think in retrospect, sees another most concretely and precisely when he views him as an incumbent in a social slot, sees him moving into the slot, occupying it at the moment and acting appropriately or not, and moving out. Primary Fox reality is, I believe, such a system of social positions that endure.

I think of my friend: "Joe (who is a father). . . ." A Fox thinks of his friend: "This father (who is Joe). . . ."I recall an incident which bears:

We left the Fox at midnight one warm September evening in 1953 to return to Chicago. Early in the evening, my wife and I had piled our gear into the car, thinking of an early start the next morning. Sol Tax, who had completed a short visit, was to drive back with us. Toward midnight, we were sitting drinking coffee in the kitchen of the farmhouse where we had lived for fifteen months. On some impulse I said, "Let's go now." Sol had no objection; Marjorie agreed; so we rounded up our two cats, the kittens of one of them, tossed them in the car, and left.

I know now why I left on that impulse. None of the Fox were about at midnight. The next morning, people would be up. Some unspoken premonition made me know that some would come around to say good-bye, that no one would know what to say or how to say it, that it would be awkward—not painful, certainly not tearful, just awkward. We left at midnight to avoid that awkward situation.

The people had known about our departure for some weeks. During that time many of the Indians had made appropriate remarks. Indeed, there had been a party at the Legion hall where friends gave us presents and one made a short speech. They said, in effect, "We're glad you came and helped us." The things they said were abstract, completely lacking in reference to what in particular had transpired: to the trip to the Bureau of Indian Affairs' regional office in Minneapolis with members of the tribal council where I had tried, but certainly failed, to help; to pouring the cement floor at the Fox American Legion post where I had only been in the way; to the trial farming venture that (as we predicted) showed no promise; to another trip to Minnesota with relatives of a Fox who had died there while visiting a group of Chippewa, to bring back the body, one of the few instances where I had clearly "helped." Especially, the farewell remarks made no reference to the mystery Fox Indians had been to me, and still were, if in much reduced measure. That is, there had been no communicated sense of the fact most salient to me, product of Western culture that I am: I, an ego, a particular organism with a history and a resulting personality, had in a host of particular ways spent some part of myself with them and was, as a result, a somewhat changed person.

"We're glad you came and helped us," they said. Their rather embarrassed utterances seemed to be rote recitations of their perception of my assigned job, my instructions on leaving the department of anthropology, of The University of Chicago: "Go out there and help the Indians." I have decided that those awkward good-byes were exactly that—recitations of my job as they perceived it. Of course it followed to my Western sense that no one had said good-bye, quite.

Thus, our departure from the Fox meant to our Western minds the end of an encounter among egos. To the Fox, the imagery seems to have been different. Certain imprecise and unnamed social slots had come to exist in virtue of the presence of "the students" in the community; but the Fox could not know what our departure meant in terms of the new social positions, they were confused, and therefore they could not decide what acts would be appropriate and gracious.

To the Fox, who thought (we are supposing) in terms of enduring organization, the logically possible meanings of our departure were three. Perhaps the new positions were to continue, and we (through correspondence and visits) were to continue as the incumbents. Or perhaps we were vacating those niches, which were to be filled by others. Or perhaps the positions themselves were to disappear with our departure. These, I judge, were critical differences to the Indians, and without this knowledge they could not decide what was appropriate.

With the few facts at their disposal, they could not know. The University of Chicago had continued research among the Fox for over five years, since the summer of 1948. The University owned a farmhouse that had served others before us and then us and was keeping it presumably to serve still others. At that time of our departure, however, none of us at Chicago knew where the next dollars were to come from and there was a great deal of thinking ahead before we would know what ought to be done next. So we were guarded about what we promised.

Among the three logical possibilities, it was conceivable that my wife and I would continue to fill, from a distance and intermittently, the new niches we had held. In small societies such niches can be established rather quickly, but they seem to require years, not months, to assume a measure of precision. Once precise, they come to carry fairly definite demands and expectations as to conduct. But these demands and expectations accrue through trial and error; they are formulated through an admixture of thought and half-conscious intuition with an eye to the work that they do, the purposes they serve. On short experience, these expectations had not yet accrued. The Fox did not know what useful or hurtful purposes we served in Fox society; we ourselves had even less knowledge about our effects. So no adequate background of experience could suggest whether the tasks of the new niches could be performed at a distance. In any event, if the niches were to continue with the present incumbents in them, what was left to require ceremonial recognition? Fox men and families were perpetually leaving to visit alien parts, but in that moving about nothing happened to social slots or their incumbents, and little note was taken.

Or our leaving could have meant that the positions themselves were finished. With this, the Fox could not possibly cope—not out of any sense of loss, necessarily, but because such a thing had rare precedent in Fox tradition. What in past experience would suggest how appropriately to mark the demise of a social niche? If motherhood should somehow cease, would the appropriate ceremony be like a funeral? A few Fox niches have gone into disuse in living memory—for example, the traditional chief and his council of clan heads were replaced (with guidance from the U.S. government) by an elected council—but about this, the Fox were still divided and confused.

Or quite possibly, our departure could have meant that we as incumbents had merely left the niches empty, but our positions would endure. Fox funerals are clearly that. Each mourner feels the emptiness of some such niche—father, uncle, and so on—and soon after a death many Fox arrange other ceremonies, ritual "adoptions," to fill in a fictitious manner the empty social slots. A large part of the ritual life of the Fox and other small societies consists precisely of such ceremonial devices for moving individuals from one social place to another; girls become women, suitors become spouses, husbands become fathers, and so on, plus all inaugurations and retirements. If the Fox could have known that this was the case, if they had sensed that our departure was like a wedding or a funeral, I suppose they would have felt the security about their intuition which is prerequisite for comfortably gracious behavior. But they could not know.

So these good friends forced themselves to go through certain motions. The motions themselves were probably learned, directly or indirectly, in a course in the government-run grade school entitled, grandly, "Etiquette" (not "American Etiquette," just "Etiquette"). Thus the form was to them strange and false, and the content sounded like, and probably was, a recitation of my formally assigned social niche as they vaguely saw it: "We're glad you came and helped."

The Fox, as I have surmised, did not often think in terms of personality; the notion appeared to be a useless encumbrance in the flow of their everyday life. The man-on-the-street notion of personality is a device to predict the behavior of others when knowledge is incomplete and time is short. In our Western lives we seldom know much about the people we must deal with and we seldom have time to wait for more knowledge. So we develop the ability to make little inductive leaps from a few past occurrences to inferences about enduring qualities of mind, to predictions of future recurrence, and then we act, taking the necessary risk. But in everyday Fox life knowledge was virtually complete and almost always there was time.

The Fox were a face-to-face community of six hundred people, most of whom lived within a radius of two miles. It followed that everyone came very close to knowing everything about everyone else: a Fox easily "knew" that another usually became more amenable when careful mention was made of his good looks. But that Fox gained no additional information or guidance by naming the other "vain," to say nothing of "narcissistic."

Further, for most of the sorts of things that had to be settled between Fox individuals, there was plenty of time. Traditionally, circumstances which required speedy judgment (as in warfare) were exceptional, and were handled exceptionally. In the usual run of traditional events, to negotiate with a man about marrying his sister, to decide whether to join with a man in a hunting party, there was time. The Fox, dealing over the generations with such unhurried events, developed habits and rules of personal conduct which were appropriate, and Fox life today is, in these crucial respects, the same.

Fox relationships were and are very cautious. A good Fox was unassuming, cautious, circumspect in his approaches to others, and in this respect most Fox most of the time were good. A Fox should never give the appearance of trying to direct another, make up his mind for him, coerce him (unless they happened to be father and son or mother's brother and nephew). Yet Fox individuals had interests and wills: a man wanted to marry another's sister, and the other may or may not want it. So a Fox pursuing his interests moved cautiously. He knew virtually everything there was to know about the other; therefore he did not try to predict to himself the other's response and then burn his bridges on the gamble that he was right. He had time, so he moved cautiously, indirectly, and the other responded with equal caution. Gradually, perhaps over weeks and months, the sentiments of each became apparent to the other, without quite being uttered. If there were a meeting of minds, the matter was made explicit and agreed to; if wills conflicted, the matter was quietly dropped (though either may later spread gossip). It was as if all Fox imagined that any instance of open, face-to-face conflict would seriously threaten the balance of the universe. Traditionally, explicit Fox thought came very close to such a view. Its cost is in time. If there is time, it is as good a way as any of getting on with the work.

Men of the West, in their everyday affairs, have little knowledge and no time, so they find the notion of personality a necessary device to predict the behavior of others. Fox had exhaustive knowledge of each other and usually time to spare, and they seemed to find the notion of personality a useless encumbrance in everyday life. They thought instead about structure; they named to themselves and to each other the Fox persons deemed to exist and brought thus to mind expected roles.

Fox social structure was elaborate and detailed, perhaps because Fox minds have long dwelt on it. The number of social persons any Fox might be outnumbered the total Fox population because any particular man was many things: father to one, husband to another; brother to a third, etc., through the whole range of male kin terms in use; in addition, he might be fellow clansman, warrior, chief or council member, etc., through a less sizable range of group memberships and offices recurrently made active according to the tasks at hand. Any single Fox was different things to different men, and even different things to the same man at different times.

The social niches of the Fox dictated such behavior as giving and receiving, ordering and deferring, as well as such unlikely things as with whom one ought (and ought not) to joke. Such thoughts, I suggest, were in the front of Fox minds as they moved through everyday Fox life: the social things one was, the social things one's fellow were, the kinds of conduct that seemed appropriate in virtue of being those things. The Fox did have psyches, of course, and must have been self-consciously aware of them. But how do a people attuned to awareness of social structure and unaccustomed to the notion of personality think about their psyches? How did a Fox visualize his "self"?

When a Western mind chances to ask "Who am I?" it must come strongly to mind that he is a man among many kinds of men. He has not always been the sort of man he is; his mind retains concrete and sometimes painful memories of the series of events in which, one after the other, his choices were made (rationally and otherwise) among competing ways of being. An unmistakable fact cannot but preoccupy his awareness: his unique history and the unique results, his unique self.

I can sense much less clearly the analogous thoughts that stood out in the mind of a Fox when he asked: "Who am I?" But it is well known that the Fox and other such small societies were traditionally homogeneous: every man's career recapitulated in all critical details the career of every other man. A Fox young man of, say, thirty-five, could see about him children who were essentially like the child he had been; he could see other young men who were in most important respects like him; he could see older men who represented the old man he would become. As a Fox looked about him, few sights or sounds would remind him of his differences from others or recall to him large choices made in his past. A Fox would remember his own life, of course, but his personal career, because it was much like the careers of others, because it was not filled with large points of career choice, was not of great significance in everyday experience and therefore was not often called to mind. The contrasts that were vividly paraded each day were between all children (past, present, and future) on the one hand, and all young men or all old men on the other; and beyond those age categories, contrasts among the several social things all the members of each age category were caused to become, each in his turn. These distinctions were timeless, enduring. A Fox had no vivid sense of becoming something new; at any moment, his sense must have been that he was living out something that had been, was, and would be.

Fox life is not quite so homogeneous today. There are alternatives that invite him, for example between competing religions. But these alternatives are not of long duration, and while they have forced very painful choices on a few, I believe that Fox mental habits have not yet caught up.

Persons who work with Indians—government officials, neighbors, anthropologists—very often remark that Indians never quite reveal themselves: no matter how long one knows most Indians, these men say, they seem to be holding back. Usually, this is explained (note again the notion of character) in terms of secretiveness or suspiciousness. I believe otherwise. Most Indians do not reveal themselves because it does not occur to them that they have unique selves to reveal. Their minds run habitually, easily, and more surely through other channels.

Perhaps when a Fox has named the many social things he is, acted them out before you, relived them in a conversation, mentioned other social things he was in the past and still others he will be in the future, he has laid his psyche (as he consciously perceives it) bare. Perhaps his offering intends to say: "There I am." But we Westerners only half comprehend that which is told and we sit waiting to hear other kinds of things. The image of the man that results seems to a Western mind to fall short of the measure of intimacy we expect among friends. Conversely, what we habitually offer, the histories of our personal proclivities, must seem strangely inadequate and irrelevant to a Fox.

Are then the Fox believable? Of course I have some confidence that I am correct in these comments about the Fox self. Even so, I do not know. Frankly, I do not. Perhaps, after all, there is an irreducible estrangement, a final incapacity to recognize oneself in a tribal or peasant other.

I have said what I could about the Fox sense of the Fox self; perhaps it may prove to approximate truth. These notions are to me newly disturbing. Thinking earlier in a different manner about different facts, we saw that the Fox community and probably most American Indian communities are structurally paralyzed. These communities were viewed as systems of imagined social niches with rules about conduct whose end was to get work done; but the systems had become rusty because they were not allowed by circumstances to run. It is disturbing to see a human community down on life: dull, listless, and disillusioned in the context of many of its local affairs. This sort of paralysis affects the webs of interlocking social niches, makes their occupancy unrewarding, impossible to fulfill, often embarrassing. Men might very well wash their hands of it all and fall back into boredom.

But what I now envisage is even more disturbing. What if it is true that an Indian's imagery of his inner being is something like what I have said? What if it is filled with awareness of all the social things he is, has been, and will be? What then if some or many or all of those social things have been rendered disappointing and unrewarding and unwanted? What then can he say when he asks himself: "Who am I?" Those young veterans were reaching out, I knew; I think now that I grossly underestimated how desperately.

Scattered here and there across the land are miserable handfuls of men, women, and children, utterly desolate, living in hovels, seemingly beyond all help other than gifts of the merest material things that keep them biologically alive. These are the remnants of the few Indian communities in which, it appears, structural paralysis has become complete. In these communities paralysis started earlier, or worked faster, or somehow went unchecked, compared to the Fox and most other Indians. Perhaps these miserable ones, are, as they appear, mere shells, their psyches emptied by the slow removal one by one of all the social things they possibly could be.

One could paralyze a white town by the device of removing all of the local work it does as a community. It would become a very dull place. But that local paralysis probably would not wreak total damage to those Western minds. When we paralyze an Indian community, we may, by that act, literally empty the minds of that people. Perhaps that is why Indians are often so desperate, and white men so uncomprehending of their desperation.

10. Three Anecdotes

Number 1.

WE LEFT the Fox in September, 1953. Over the ensuing few years my wife and I went occasionally to the Fox community to visit. In August, 1955, for example, we attended the Pow-wow. Again, as in previous years, we camped down at the Pow-wow grounds, watched many of the performances from behind the scenes (my wife danced with the Fox women, as usual), and we visited with old acquaintances, especially over coffee around the campfires late into the night. Many of these Fox had long since ceased to be strangers. Conversation came easily, and silences without conversation were also easy. We happened to bring with us on that trip my wife's sister, and we introduced her around.

On the third evening, rather late, we were sitting around a fire, drinking coffee and chatting idly with Tom Smith (who has since died, too soon, in his early fifties) and other Fox. During one of our comfortable lulls, Tom looked rather pointedly at my sister-in-law, then at my wife, then turned to me and said, "They look very much alike." I thought I saw a flicker of humor in his eyes, but no meaning registered. Some moments passed. Again, Tom looked deliberately at the two women and again turned to me, "They sure do look alike." (A short pause.) "I'll bet if it were dark some night, you might even make a mistake."

In fact, the two women do look alike; the rakish look in Tom Smith's eye left no doubt as to what he intended; my first fleeting response was awkward embarrassment, I suppose. But then I remembered: sisters-in-law. Indeed, the major shapes of Fox social structure flashed through my mind and the ways those arrangements of personnel have been bolstered and sustained over the many Fox generations. Of course the sexual allusion lost any coarseness it might otherwise have had. I laughed, Tom broke into chuckles, my wife grinned. Quiet laughter spread through the small group, except my wife's puzzled sister, until we told her later about Fox joking, about how Fox sisters-in-law were potential wives, and all that.

This that we have with the Fox is not quite intimate friendship, but being among these Indians is now, at the very least, a comfortable way to spend an evening.

Number 2.

In late August, 1968, after some eleven years residence on the West Coast and abroad, we again visited the Fox, joined now by our three children.

We drove into the Fox community. The roads were still

unpaved, still dusty. The community looked generally some-what greener than we remembered and, judging from the appearances of the houses, a bit more prosperous. We drove into the homesite of a family with whom my wife had been especially close. There were cheerful, quiet greetings all around, much comment about the children, some idle conversation, then this familiar sentence: "The government is trying to take away the fourth, fifth, and sixth grades of our school (what had happened to the seventh?), to make the kids go to Tama."

But wait.

Number 2½.

A few weeks later the Fox called and sustained a student boycott, out of that got a court hearing, and won. To reverse the French adage: the more things are the same, the more they change.

Number 3.

This is an Indian joke for Indian readers, and for action anthropologists a morality tale. Others may read on as they wish, at their own risk.

Long ago, it is said, there was a young warrior who had received no power. This warrior had not received a power because he had not sought a power; he had never fasted, never gone alone into the hills, never made himself pitiable to the Spirit or to any of the Powers. Therefore, it is said, the Spirit and the Powers did not see him, did not pity him, did not come to him, did not give him power.

This warrior, it is said, did not seek a power, because he wanted a special power, a power different from the powers other warriors had. Many young men had buffalo power for hunting, wind power for gambling, wildcat power for war; many had these powers. This warrior, it is said, wished for a different power. But, it is said, he had not yet been able to think of a different power, so he did not fast or go into the hills alone, and he had no power.

One day, it is said, he was sitting, sad and alone. And his great idea came to him: he would seek mosquito power. He had never heard of a man with mosquito power. He would seek mosquito power and become a great man among his people.

That very day, it is said, the young warrior walked off into the hills alone. He found a swampy place. He took off his clothes, down to his breech clout and moccasins. He lay down on the bare earth and all that day thought only of Mosquito.

Two days, it is said, he lay there, hardly moving, thinking only of Mosquito. It was cold and damp. He had no food. His body was bitten by mosquitoes until it was almost raw. But he had no vision.

The third day, it is said, he pleaded with the Spirit, "Am I not pitiable; take pity on me." And he pleaded with Mosquito, "Am I not pitiable; take pity on me." But there was no vision. His body had become bloody from the bites; he had not eaten; he could hardly tell the difference between sleeping and wakefulness. But, it is said, there was no vision.

On the fourth day, it is said, he pleaded with the Spirit and he pleaded with Mosquito, all day on his knees, without ceasing: "Indeed, am I not pitiable; indeed, take pity on me; indeed, come to me; indeed, give me power." But through the day, it is said, there was no vision, no power came, and at sunset the young man collapsed, exhausted.

At last, it is said, dusk settled, night mists began to rise from the swamp, and out of the mists, it is said, Mosquito came. Mosquito, it is said, was bigger than a man, with great hairy legs, huge green eyes. Mosquito came toward the young warrior with long, silent steps, on those great hairy legs, came within a few feet, and stood silent, fixing the warrior with those huge green eyes, it is said. The young warrior with his last strength struggled to his knees. "Great Spirit," he said, "You have pitied me! Mosquito, you have pitied me! Mosquito, you have come! Mosquito, give me power!"

Mosquito, it is said, stood silent for many minutes, not moving except for those great green eyes which looked first at the warrior's haggard face, then at his bloody, wasted body, back to the warrior's face. Then, it is said, Mosquito trembled all over, and, it is said, he spoke. "Indeed, you are pitiable. Indeed, the Great Spirit has pitied you. Indeed, I have pitied you. Indeed, I have come to you."

Then Mosquito, it is said, again became silent. The young warrior, it is said, could not speak. He waited. Many minutes he waited. Then, it is said, Mosquito trembled more fiercely than before, until the ground shook with the trembling and, it is said, he spoke: "But, friend, us mosquitoes ain't got no power." It is said.

Acknowledgments

I n 1952, very early in my graduate student career, I began
to know the Fox Indians of Iowa; I, like others before
and after, was sent to the Fox community for field training, in accordance with the sink-or-swim theory of making
anthropologists. I began then also to know well certain fellow
anthropologists (then fellow students) and especially to
know our teacher in this work, Dr. Sol Tax; all were of The
University of Chicago. Some five student years passed, and I
left Chicago in 1957. Many more years have since passed.
Today, my associations with those Indians and those anthropologists are not ended, but distance has much reduced com-
munication among us and has perhaps allowed the experience
of those years to assume the increment of meaning that

detachment often gives. So I have asked myself, "What of possible truth and importance did we learn?"

These few pages are the answer I am able to give, but it is well to add something about some of the persons who permitted me to work with them. Those student years were spent doing and thinking about what Sol Tax has called action anthropology, a form of social research in which one sets out to help and to learn, simultaneously and with equal emphasis. There were several projects, large and small, in which we tried to help and learn, but most of our thought and effort was spent in the small community of six hundred Fox Indians in Iowa. For my own part, I became mainly involved in the activities of the Fox veterans of World War II, which provided occasions in which I might, just possibly, have been of some help, but occasions in which I certainly learned. The Fox put their stamp on action anthropology, and perhaps action anthropology put some stamp on the Fox. So my teachers were the anthropologists and the Indians, the group who worked together thinking about the Indians and about the neighbors of Indians (not excluding ourselves). An account of the Fox program, distinguished perhaps by its candor, is available in the volume *Documentary History of the Fox Project: A Program in Action Anthropology, directed by Sol Tax*, edited by myself, Robert McC. Netting, and Lisa Redfield Peattie, and published by the Department of Anthropology of The University of Chicago in 1960.

Sol Tax has a mind that firmly handles complex scientific reasoning, but a mind that must also reach out to the infinitely more complex world of affairs, and he has unlimited energy. The rest of us in our work among the Fox and others were typically enmeshed and preoccupied at any moment in some narrow inquiry leading to some tentative utilization of knowledge gained; the tendency was for the two parts of our efforts, learning and helping, to get segregated as discrete activities, against our will and in violation of our own considered principles. Sol Tax held the strands of activity together. When one of us, so engaged, was preoccupied with the gathering of particular facts, it was usually Sol Tax who would imagine some form of practical assistance to the community that would reveal the facts, probably more quickly or more completely. Or if one of us was swamped with the details of some practical project, it was usually Sol Tax who would remember to inquire what, out of that activity, was being learned, and he would usually see some different way of performing the same service so as to learn more. He taught us, that is, a way of research-and-assistance that is both personally rewarding and scientifically productive.

Robert Rietz was doing anthropological research in the Fox community in 1948 and 1949, before I arrived, and after working some three years in North Dakota with the Bureau of Indian Affairs, he returned and was again with the Fox from 1955 to 1958. Beginning in 1955, he and a handful of Fox Indians started to do something about the Fox future; they began from scratch and built the beginning of a little industry in the community. It was Rietz more than any other person who forced me to recognize the significance of the facts of structural paralysis discussed in Chapter 7; that chapter is the most important, in. practical terms, of these pages.

Robert Thomas, whose insights are unusually sure, was with us in virtually all our work, bringing his experience among Indian tribes in the Southwest and elsewhere across the land and his special experience with the Cherokees of Oklahoma. Leonard Borman worked with the Penobscot Indians of Maine and later with the fabulous Kalmuks, Mongols displaced from Russia and currently living in and around Philadelphia. Lisa Redfield Peattie and Walter B. Miller worked with the Fox with Rietz, and Steven

Polgar worked there later with me. The total group over the years was larger, but I have mentioned these because I can recall specific times when each has pressed my thoughts in good directions they would not otherwise have taken.

To all the Fox Indians I am indebted, and to some thirty of them very deeply indebted. They, together, showed us, so far as we were able to learn, what it means to be an Indian. The Fox knew who they were, where they had been, and, when inconsequentials are stripped away, where they intended to go. They were good teachers and good fellow students. I name no individuals here out of regard for their personal privacy.

The thinking of these anthropologists and Indians is in these pages. Perhaps they will not always be delighted with what their thoughts, moving through my head and there joining others, have become. So I express to all of them my thanks and great indebtedness, and also my apologies.

No doubt my largest debt of all is to my wife, Marjorie Dodd Gearing, who worked with me. She and I are jointly indebted to the Edward Rosheims of Tama, who helped make our fifteen months most pleasant.

The Emil Schwarzhaupt Foundation generously supported our work among the Fox from 1955 to its conclusion. Everyone connected with that research feels most deeply appreciates the Foundation's generosity and the gracious manner in which it was administered by Carl Tscheranson.

Fred Gearing

The Fox

Some Fox . . . .

...and their Tama neighbors.

The Fox community school . . .

. . . and two Fox grandmothers making "fry bread" for a school picnic.

*Western presumption: Indian patience
(author and friend, 1952)*

A ritual-adoption ceremonial feast.